teach
yourself

coaching

teach®
yourself

coaching
amanda vickers and
steve bavister

For UK order enquiries: please contact Bookpoint Ltd, 130 Milton Park, Abingdon, Oxon OX14 4SB. Telephone: +44 (0) 1235 827720. Fax: +44 (0) 1235 400454. Lines are open 09.00–18.00, Monday to Saturday, with a 24-hour message answering service. Details about our titles and how to order are available at www.teachyourself.co.uk

For USA order enquiries: please contact McGraw-Hill Customer Services, PO Box 545, Blacklick, OH 43004-0545, USA. Telephone: 1-800-722-4726. Fax: 1-614-755-5645.

For Canada order enquiries: please contact McGraw-Hill Ryerson Ltd, 300 Water St, Whitby, Ontario L1N 9B6, Canada. Telephone: 905 430 5000. Fax: 905 430 5020.

Long renowned as the authoritative source for self-guided learning – with more than 40 million copies sold worldwide – the **teach yourself** series includes over 300 titles in the fields of languages, crafts, hobbies, business, computing and education.

British Library Cataloguing in Publication Data: a catalogue record for this title is available from the British Library.

Library of Congress Catalog Card Number: on file.

First published in UK 2005 by Hodder Arnold, 338 Euston Road, London, NW1 3BH.

First published in US 2005 by Contemporary Books, a Division of the McGraw-Hill Companies, 1 Prudential Plaza, 130 East Randolph Street, Chicago, IL 60601 USA.

The **teach yourself** name is a registered trade mark of Hodder Headline Ltd.

Copyright © 2005 Amanda Vickers and Steve Bavister

Typeset by Transet Limited, Coventry, England.
Printed in Great Britain for Hodder Education, a division of Hodder Headline, 338 Euston Road, London NW1 3BH, by Cox & Wyman Ltd, Reading, Berkshire.

Hodder Headline's policy is to use papers that are natural, renewable and recyclable products and made from wood grown in sustainable forests. The logging and manufacturing processes are expected to conform to the environmental regulations of the country of origin.

Impression number 10 9 8 7 6 5 4 3 2 1
Year   2010 2009 2008 2007 2006 2005

contents

01

coaching today

In this chapter you will learn:
- what attracts people to become coaches
- about the reality of coaching
- about coaching in companies
- why coaching is becoming increasingly popular
- what coaching is all about
- about the benefits of coaching.

The coaching boom

It's an explosion. A boom. An upsurge. A groundswell. However you describe it, interest in coaching has grown enormously in recent years. The shelves in bookshops heave with the multitude of titles on the subject. It's regularly featured in magazines, newspapers and in TV. And it's become something of a buzzword in business. No wonder, then, that it's caught the interest of so many people. Since you're reading this book, you're almost certainly one of them. Maybe you've seen advertisements for life coaching courses that suggest you can earn a good living while doing something rewarding. Perhaps you dream of escaping the rat race, taking your nose away from the grindstone and your back away from the wheel. Or maybe you work in a company where you coach your team – or would like to start doing so. You realize it's an important management skill these days, and one you need to develop if you're going to get the short and long-term results you deserve.

It could be you work in an HR or Training Department and are looking for information to help you support line managers in creating a coaching culture – an environment where everyone learns from each other as a matter of course and where individual, team and organizational goals are integrated. This is increasingly becoming a must-have rather than a nice-to-have for organizations that want to achieve sustainable success. If this is what you're after you'll find lots of useful material to support you in developing the skills of your people but we do not have space here to explain the organizational context in depth. Perhaps you just want to learn more about one of the most powerful tools for personal and professional growth around – and the benefits it can have in all areas of life. Whatever your reason, we've filled this book full of essential information that will help you understand the theory and practice of coaching.

Why become a coach?

As with anything, people have different reasons for getting into coaching. Here are three of the most common.

Fulfilment and satisfaction

Coaching can be extremely fulfilling and satisfying. It's an enormous privilege to be able to work with people on the most intimate and important issues in their lives. This is true whether you're coaching inside a company or work as an independent life or executive coach.

People often decide to become coaches because they want to make a difference in the world. There's nothing like the feeling you get when you've supported someone in making a change, assisted them in dealing with an issue, helped them achieve a goal or aided them in simply being happier.

People seek out coaching for many different reasons, but generally there's a gap between how things are and how they want them to be. The coach's role is to support them in bridging it. They might want to earn more money, enrich their relationships, have a more balanced lifestyle or make progress in their career.

Coaching also operates at a much deeper level, with clients frequently developing far greater self-awareness and sensitivity. They end up taking more responsibility for themselves, are more motivated, and are better able to regulate their behaviour – or, as we now describe this cluster of qualities, they become more emotionally intelligent.

One of the bonuses of becoming a coach is that in the process of working with others you develop these qualities as well.

Reflection on the benefits of coaching from a client

Coaching has helped me to get clarity over what's important to me in my life and work and I have noticed that I have moved forward with my goals much faster than I had expected. I have a sense that I have changed in a number of smaller ways how I go about doing things now, that I hardly even notice anymore because they have become part of me. There are a number of tangible differences about the way I work. I am much more organized and use my time more effectively than I did before. Perhaps the greatest change though, has been the insights I have gained into what motivates me and what is important to me about the relationships I have with others. I am much gentler with myself than I used to be and that seems to have a positive effect on the way I am with other people.

Coaching can be financially rewarding

Compared to many lines of work, coaching can also be financially rewarding. Rates vary considerably, but it's perfectly possible to earn as much in an hour or two as some people make in a whole day. It's not hard to see why that prospect might be appealing!

Independence

Some people who want to be coaches are drawn to the idea of being their own boss. Instead of having someone else tell them what to do they call the shots. They want to be able to quit the rat race and paddle their own canoe – working only when they want to, making their own decisions.

The reality of coaching

However, the reality of coaching – like many things in life – doesn't always live up to the promise. The last thing we want to do is pour cold water on your hopes and dreams. But we do feel we have a responsibility to give you a true picture of the world of coaching.

The good news is that all the media coverage of coaching has created and stimulated demand, and up and down the country thousands of sessions take place every week. People know that it's possible to have a more enjoyable, fulfilling life, and are aware that coaching is one way of achieving it. So, prospective clients are actively seeking it out.

The bad news is that demand is not as great as the advertisements for coach training companies often suggest. And there are now a great many coaches in the market, so it's an extremely competitive field. It can take some time to build up a coaching business to the point where you can pay the bills from it. If you've been thinking of quitting your job and setting up in business we suggest you read this book first.

What is needed

Coaching skills alone aren't enough

One of the key things to understand is that coaching skills alone are not enough. You also need to be self-motivated have a knack for business if you're going to make a success of working independently. In fact, someone who's not particularly skilled at coaching but excellent at marketing will do better than a talented coach who can't sell. On average self-employed coaches need to spend a third of their time winning business – so it's an essential part of the skill-set.

And while you'll obviously be working with people – you'll be seeing clients face-to-face and speaking to them on the phone – coaching can, to a degree, be a solitary business. You'll most likely be working on your own, rather than as part of a team. That doesn't suit everyone. And when you're focused on promotion you'll often be alone.

You also don't get paid when you have a day or week off like you would if you were employed. And when you run your own business the responsibility for getting everything done rests with you.

Stamina and courage
After that rather sobering 'reality check', we'd like to balance things a little by saying say that if you do have the stamina, courage and skills to make the break, running your own coaching business really can be a dream come true. Chapter 4 looks at ways you can get started and Chapter 19 examines aspects of marketing and finance.

Coaching in companies

Things are simpler, in some ways when it comes to companies. Many now recognize the value of coaching as one of the most cost-effective ways of developing staff. Instead of 'sheep dipping' everyone by putting them through training courses they use coaching that's tailored to meet individual needs. This is especially valuable with more experienced people who've already attended every course going. The benefits to businesses are many and wide-ranging, including:

- increased business performance
- rapid staff development
- improved retention of key staff
- superior productivity and customer service
- better motivation and deeper commitment to the company
- enhanced leadership capabilities.

Business has embraced coaching in two main ways:

1 By expecting managers to coach their teams as part of their standard skill set
2 By bringing in external coaches to work with people at a senior level.

Chapters 5 and 6 will look at these areas in detail. Some of the changes that have contributed to this in the business world are an increased emphasis on leadership skills, a move towards flatter organizations and remote working, and executives find it useful to have someone who can act as a sounding board.

Distrust of coaching in the corporate world has all but evaporated, with most of those who receive it realizing that it's of enormous advantage to them in developing their careers – rather than implemented because they're failing in some way. Many companies now have a 'coaching culture', or are thinking about setting one up, so that everyone benefits whatever level they're at.

Exciting times

These are exciting times for coaching. There are those who said it wouldn't last – that it was just a fashion or fad. But its enduring popularity has proved that forecast wrong. Coaching is here to stay – and we believe it will continue to grow in acclaim and recognition over the years to come. And you can be part of it. Whether you decide to pursue a vocation as a coach, or prefer to use some of the skills to enhance various areas of your life, you will make a difference in the world – not only for those with whom you come into contact but also for yourself.

What you can do

- Talk to other coaches and ask them to fill you in on what it is really like to be a coach.
- Review your own reasons for becoming a coach or for improving your coaching skills.
- Consider the downsides to becoming an independent coach and how you might overcome them.

02 natural coaching

In this chapter you will learn:
- that many people are natural coaches
- that coaching is a special kind of conversation
- about the qualities of good coaches
- if you have the characteristics and personality to make a good coach.

People are natural coaches

Chris is a successful manager with a team of twenty. In the main, they're a motivated, enthusiastic bunch who seem to enjoy what they do – although that doesn't stop them complaining, given the chance. There's a buzz in the office and it can seem a bit chaotic, but everything gets done without any need to 'crack the whip' – and they always achieve and often exceed their targets. How does Chris do it? One of his secrets is that he makes time every day to say hello to each person in the team. That's not always easy as there seems to be a million things clamouring for his attention from the moment he sets foot in the door. But finding time for his people is really important to him. And, though he wouldn't care to admit it, in a way they're like family and he wants to do the best for them. Whenever time allows, Chris loves to chat with members of his team. He's genuinely interested, not just in how they feel about work, but in what's going on in the rest of their lives – and, because they respect and trust him, they tend to be open and honest in what they say. In fact, they sometimes seek him out and use him as a sounding board – because the supportive way in which he challenges their thinking helps them to become clear about their issues. Only occasionally, when things are really frantic, does he try to solve the problem for them or tell them what to do. He encourages them to come up with their own solutions. Not surprisingly, Chris is a popular boss and his team will be sorry to see him go when he gets promoted.

Some people are natural coaches. They have an easy manner and quickly 'connect' with others. They're interested in what makes people tick and – more than that – they're curious, inquisitive even. But it's curiosity that comes from the heart: a willingness, a desire to help people around them become the best they can. They have a knack of asking the right question at the right time and supporting others in working things out for themselves, knowing that in doing so they'll learn and grow in the process.

Sarah has had a variety of jobs and done well in most of them, but none has been really satisfying. She dreams of doing something more fulfilling, something where she can 'make a difference'. People tell her she's a 'good listener'. Both at work and outside they confide in her at the drop of a hat – even complete strangers she meets on the train! Maybe it's because she doesn't seem inclined to judge or criticize. Sarah loves to let them talk. It seems to help them understand what's going on. Every now and then she'll ask a question or make a comment, but she tends to keep her opinions to herself. She wonders whether there's a way in which she can turn this 'passion' she has for people into a way of earning a living.

Because they respect other people, natural coaches accept them as they are. They don't foist their own views and ideas on someone who is grappling with an issue. They believe it's better for them to come to their own conclusion, since only they know what's truly right for them. Of course, people do get 'stuck' in their thinking and can often go round in circles. That's when natural coaches will raise a pertinent query that allows the individual to consider new choices and possibilities for themselves.

If you think back over your life so far, you'll find examples of where you've given encouragement to others and believed in them, even when they doubted themselves. You may find yourself recalling times in a work situation when someone was seeking promotion and you asked them questions to help clarify what they wanted. It could be that someone you know needed someone to listen while they poured out their thoughts and feelings about some big change they faced in their life such as divorce, separation, retirement or children leaving home.

As you reflect on your experiences, you may recall relationships or situations where this happens more naturally or often than others. It could be with close friends, your partner or spouse, family, children or the people you play sports with. You might find you're thinking of people you meet at your gym, church or at the local amateur dramatic society. At work, you may find that people come to you for help in identifying the next step in their career.

Natural coaching can and does take place at any time. Whenever someone presents you with an issue, you can find yourself working with them to help identify a solution that fits for them. So you've probably been coaching in a natural way for most of your life already.

You might also have remembered some of the times when you were on the receiving end of natural coaching. Perhaps you were puzzled or confused about something or didn't know what direction to take and someone you know asked you just the right question at the right time. When that happens, you often find the right solution for you just pops into your mind and everything suddenly feels straightforward and simple. If you've had some experience of coaching others already you could be reflecting on some of the moments when your clients inspired you through their ability to make changes in their lives. Changes, whether in your personal or professional life, are often easier to come to terms with if you're able to explore what the change means to you with someone you trust. All of these experiences are really just different examples of people using coaching skills in their day-to-day lives.

Coaching is more than conversation

Coaching is conversation – but a special kind of conversation. Coaches speak and listen with a number of aims in mind. They're motivated by helping their clients achieve their goals, deal with their issues, clarify what's important to them – and a whole lot more. Many people do this naturally out of a genuine desire to understand and help. Others seek to shower the person with advice – much like scattering seeds in the hope that one will fall on fertile ground and take root. Rather than forcing a solution on someone, coaching involves unearthing their own answer or way forward from within. Coaching conversations empower people, and support them in being their best.

> As Ruth reflects on her decision to become a coach she says, 'I feel that I've been coaching for most of my life in a way. In every job I've done, I've enjoyed the people side the most. The only difference now is that I have a name for what I've been doing – coaching. It's part of who I am. I find myself coaching in all kinds of situations – formally and informally. Whether it's been meeting customers or collaborating with a team on a project, I've always got the biggest buzz from helping people to achieve things.' Ruth's clients say she has a real ability to put people at ease. She's not totally sure how she does it because it feels to her to be an ability she's been unconsciously honing for most of her life.

Can anyone become a coach?

Can anyone become a coach? Yes – and no. In the same way that anyone can learn to play the piano, but certain people have a talent for the instrument and take to it easily, so some people develop the skills of coaching more readily and become accomplished more quickly.

Given that coaching is essentially just sitting chatting to someone, either face to face or by telephone, you'd think anyone could do it. But experience shows that you need a particular mindset to be effective. If you're not naturally a 'people person'– and are more comfortable dealing with tasks and projects – you may struggle to achieve success in the coaching world, with clients feeling you're a little 'cold'.

Even if you acquire coaching skills the people you coach with will quickly detect you're not really that interested in them. If the opposite is true, and you love working with people and delight in seeing them blossom and grow, you're well on the way to being an accomplished practitioner.

Coaches, though, come in all shapes, ages, races and personalities, and enter the profession by many different routes. Some make a switch from something completely unrelated, such as sales or retail, in search of a more fulfilling way of earning a living. Others simply want to develop their coaching skills to be more effective in an existing occupation or role. It can be helpful if you have a background in business (and important if you want to be an Executive Coach – see Chapter 5), an interest in psychology and personal development, or even a spiritual dimension to your life if that's important to some of your clients, but in practice none of this really matters. Wherever you start from, in terms of experience and natural ability, you can make it if you're determined and work at it.

The qualities of a good coach

What qualities does a good coach need? Well, to a degree it's a question of what kind of coach they want to be. As we'll see in Chapter 3, there are many types of coaching and these require different talents. That said, the underlying skill set is pretty much the same whatever approach you take. We don't claim our list is definitive, but you'll certainly find it a useful guide and something to aspire to. You obviously won't have all these qualities – we don't know any coach who does – so don't be daunted by what you read.

Awareness and observation

If you want to be an effective coach you can't just go round sleep-walking your way through life – you need to be aware of what's going on in the world around you. In particular, it's important to be aware of other people as unique individuals, each with their own dreams, fears, talents, issues etc. – because that's essentially the raw material of coaching. It's also useful to be observant, noticing patterns and themes in what your clients say and do – or don't say and don't do.

Curiosity and patience

A coach's job is to help clients explore their issues. But rather than thinking they understand or know the answer already, they ask questions in a spirit of genuine curiosity. It's more or less essential to be a good listener – the client should do most of the talking – and patience is a virtue well worth cultivating.

Empathy and building rapport

When a coach is empathic a 'safe space' is created where the person can open up fully and talk honestly about how they feel. And when you have a genuine interest in the person you're coaching you'll connect quickly with them, establishing and maintaining rapport easily.

Respect, trust and integrity

It's also essential to have respect for the person you're coaching and create a climate of trust. What clients want is integrity – someone who does what they say they'll do, who walks the talk, and can be relied upon to be confidential.

Clarity of thought, confidence and approachability

If you have excellent clarity of thought that will help your clients enormously. Sometimes they'll come to a session confused, looking to you to help and guide them through it. Appearing confident will make them feel they're in safe hands, but being prepared to admit mistakes and being human will implicitly give your clients permission to be human themself.

Solution-focus and detachment

While other people's lives, and problems can be fascinating, if you want to be an effective coach you need to be solution focused – working with them to get to where they want to go to, rather than looking at what might have 'gone wrong' in the past. Remaining detached means the coach doesn't get caught up in the person's 'story' and retains an objective perspective.

Positivity and creativity

When a coach has a positive, optimistic outlook it tends to rub off on their clients and makes things seem possible. That opens the door to approaching issues in a creative and original way.

Challenging, honesty and encouragement

Good coaches are also prepared to challenge their clients to be their best and are honest and direct in their feedback. They're comfortable with risk and encourage people to step outside their comfort zone and 'raise the bar'.

Compassion, open-mindedness and admiration

One of the most important qualities any coach can have is compassion, accepting their clients just as they are, with tolerance and without prejudice. When you're non-judgemental about them and open-minded about the decisions they make and the actions they take, something magical often happens.

We've heard some coaches say they don't like some of their clients. In our view, they should not be coaching them. We believe you have to admire your client in some way, to be able to 'hold them big', to believe in their ability to achieve what they want to do, if you're to be an effective coach for them.

Relaxed approach

Being easy-going and relaxed rather than being earnest and serious when coaching will assist your clients in playing around with new ideas, which means getting better results.

Self-awareness

One of the most amazing qualities about being human is our capacity for self-awareness. We're able to reflect on our inner experience and be conscious of our own consciousness.

If you know yourself well, are comfortable 'in your skin', reasonably well sorted, and emotionally stable, you're likely to make a good coach. This is extremely important as you'll sometimes find yourself working with people who are experiencing personal difficulties.

Authenticity

Above all great coaches are real and authentic. They're not acting as they think a coach should act. They're being themselves first and foremost, and then coaching.

Activity

Assess your potential to be a great coach using the list below of good coaching qualities. Rank yourself between 0 and 4, where 0 is 'I'm absolutely rubbish at this' to 4 'I'm a real hot shot – the best there could be'. If you're somewhere in the middle you're likely to give yourself a score of 2. Next, add up all the numbers and arrive at a total.

Aware (of self and others)	Comfortable with risk
Encouraging	Honest
Non-judgemental	Positive
Empathic	Enquiring/Curious
Patient	Open-minded
Good listener	Creative
Observant	Solution-focused
Able to create and maintain rapport	Detached
Warm and compassionate	Clear thinking
Respect others	Confident
Demonstrates integrity	Emotionally stable
Challenging	Easy-going and relaxed
	Authentic and real

If you scored more than 80

Wow! You are truly gifted and destined to become a master coach – unless, of course, you're one already. Either that or you're not as self-aware as you think you are! Even people who are aiming for 'sainthood' have a few areas they can improve on. Take a good look at your scores and if you're satisfied your adding up is right home in on what you have to do to completely earn that halo.

If you scored between 61 and 80

You obviously have a solid set of skills and should have no problem doing an effective job of coaching. There's no room for complacency though. How can you raise the bar even higher for yourself? After all that's what you'll be asking your clients to do. Examine your scores closely and work out which hurdles you've yet to leap over.

If you scored between 41 and 60

You've got some of the qualities of a good coach but may need to strengthen others. Have a look at your scores and see if you can identify any clusters of characteristics that can be improved. Maybe it's your patience or listening that lets you down or perhaps you need to be empathic, warm and compassionate. As you read through the book bear in mind the qualities you need to work on and everything will slot into place.

If you scored between 21 and 40

It doesn't mean you can't coach but there's some work to do. You have some of the skills of a natural coach. You may want to reflect on whether you're good at being brutally honest or just hard on yourself. Reading this book will help a lot and it's going to be important for you to complete all the exercises. If you really want to be good at coaching you'll get there.

If you scored between 20 or less

Don't give up your day job! We don't think you're cut out for all this 'pink and fluffy' stuff somehow. Coaching isn't for everyone. Maybe there's another job that's better suited to your talents. That doesn't mean of course you can't use coaching skills – but coaching as a profession probably isn't your forte.

However you scored, you'll have a useful starting point for where to focus your attention in developing your skills as a coach.

What you can do

- Start to notice when you or other people are coaching naturally. What is it that makes it 'natural coaching'?
- Ask someone you trust and who knows you well to assess the list of coaching qualities on your behalf and then compare your score with theirs.

03

understanding coaching

In this chapter you will learn:
- how coaching originated
- the diverse approaches people take to coaching
- how coaching differs from other consulting professions
- about different types of coaching
- of common myths about coaching.

To get ahead you need a coach

When tennis players hold the Wimbledon trophy aloft, having just won the final, they do not celebrate alone. When a football team beats all comers to claim the World Cup, someone else partners in their success. Virtually every leading sportsperson has their own coach. It is the same for pop stars, who have vocal, dance and style coaches, and more besides.

Why do they bother? The answer is quite simple: they bother because coaching works. Not just in terms of physical development or learning new skills, but also in terms of mental and emotional preparation. This can be what makes a difference with almost anything a person attempts to achieve. To get ahead, you need to get a coach.

A brief history of coaching

The origin of the word 'coach' is both interesting and surprising. It comes from the French *coche* and derives originally from a small Hungarian town called Kòcs where the first coach/wagon was built in the sixteenth century. Before long the noun became a verb, and people who transported others from one place to another started describing what they did as 'coaching'. Then, by one of those quirks often seen in language, the word was borrowed to describe the work of tutors in the field of education who 'carried' their pupils through to their exams.

The association of coaching with sport took root at the end of the nineteenth century when US college students began to have coaches, as well as managers, to support them in achieving their best. It was a former tennis player, Tim Gallwey, who laid the foundations for coaching as we know it today. In his seminal 1974 book, *The Inner Game of Tennis*, he put forward a revolutionary notion – that the best way to help someone become a better player was not to make suggestions but to ask questions that would enable them to learn from their own experience. This is the essence of coaching as it is practised today. It was also discovered that the most effective coaches were not, contrary to what you might expect, experienced in the sport.

These principles of coaching were soon being adopted by corporate America, and they were brought to Europe by one of Gallwey's students, Sir John Whitmore, with the publication of his influential book, *Coaching for Performance* (1999).

However, it was the foundation of Coach University in 1992 by Thomas Leonard, a financial planner from San Francisco, that really put coaching on the map, and many other coach training schools all over the world followed in its wake. Since then, coaching has continued to grow. A survey conducted in 2004 by the Chartered Institute of Personnel and Development (CIPD) showed that 79 per cent of businesses use coaching.

Approaches to coaching

The coaching industry is still in its infancy. There is no regulation or standardization and, with so many different approaches to coaching, there is a certain amount of confusion. The aim of this chapter is to bring some clarity to the situation by discussing the various definitions of some of the approaches.

The Co-active model

While there is no right or wrong when it comes to coaching, we believe that in current best practice it's a collaborative process in which clients discover answers for themselves through the use of questions.

The Co-active coaching model is described in detail in the book by Whitworth et al. called *Co-active Coaching: New Skills for Coaching People Towards Success in Work and Life* (1998), which is an essential read for anyone serious about coaching. There are four cornerstones to the approach:

1 The client is naturally creative, resourceful and whole.
2 Coaching addresses the client's whole life.
3 The agenda comes from the client.
4 The relationship is a designed alliance.

This approach presupposes that the client is not 'broken' – they work perfectly, and it's not the coach's responsibility to fix them. The client is an expert on themselves and the skill of the coach, and their role, is in allowing the person to come up with their own solutions. This doesn't mean the coach brings nothing to the party – they have methods, exercises and questions that help the person move forwards. Nevertheless, the coach's skills are based around processes, not solutions.

Not everyone subscribes to the Co-active coaching model. Some people are perfectly happy to suggest things to their clients, give them solutions, and even help them in practical ways by doing things for them. Between these two extremes there is a middle ground where many coaches end up – always working to the client's agenda and principally asking questions, but being prepared to share their experience and insight when it will assist them.

Directive versus non-directive

Coaching can, therefore, be directive, with the coach acting as expert and providing solutions to their client's issues, or non-directive, where the aim is to draw out the client's own understanding.

Directive/Non-Directive

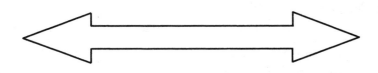

Directive
Telling, training, teaching

Non-Directive
Listening, questioning, challenging

figure 1 Directive and non-directive coaching

This book takes the view that once you start telling, training and teaching people, this is not actually coaching.

Sample dialogue
Directive coaching

Coach: So, you want to feel confident about speaking in public?

Client: Yes, that's right

Coach: Well the most important thing is to prepare really well and create a well-thought out structure that people will be able to follow easily.

Client: Where do I start?

Coach: I suggest you start by being clear about the purpose of your talk and the message you want the audience to get.

When coaches use a directive style, they make numerous suggestions for their client based on their knowledge and expertise. Directive language does have its place; if you don't know how to operate a video recorder, and want to be able to, a non-directive coaching approach won't get you very far.

Coach: So, you want to know how to programme a video recorder?
Client: Yes, that's right.
Coach: What would you say is the first step?
Client: If I knew that I wouldn't need to ask!

In this case, it's a lot easier to give the person instructions.

In non-directive coaching, the responsibility lies primarily with the person being coached – not the coach. In this book, the approach is largely non-directive.

Sample dialogue
Non-directive coaching

Coach: So, you want to feel confident about speaking in public?
Client: Yes, that's right.
Coach: What stops you?
Client: I start to feel nervous.
Coach: At what point does that happen?
Client: It builds up all through the day before – especially if I haven't had enough time to prepare.
Coach: So, when you are prepared you don't feel as nervous?
Client: It certainly helps but I'm still nervous until I've got going and said a few words.
Coach: What would help you get off to a good start?
Client: (Pauses) Perhaps if I worked out precisely what I'm going to say at the beginning I wouldn't be worrying so much about making a mistake.

A non-directive approach leaves the client feeling more resourceful and confident about coming up with their own solutions in future situations.

How is coaching different?

It is important to be clear about the distinction between coaching and other interventions such as mentoring, training, consulting, counselling and therapy. In each case, the practitioner is working one on one with the client, but there are significant differences in both practice and philosophy.

Mentoring

The word 'mentoring' originates from Greek mythology, where it is said that Odysseus entrusted his home and the education of his son to his friend Mentor. 'Tell him all you know,' said Odysseus, hence the common understanding of mentoring as 'passing on experience and knowledge'. Widely used in business, mentoring provides a mechanism by which senior managers can pass on their wisdom, 'tricks of the trade' and short-cuts to success – helping to shape their protégé's values and beliefs in a positive way. Unlike coaching, where the emphasis is on getting the person to come up with their own solutions, mentors often give advice and guidance, although most do use coaching skills as well.

Training

Training is defined in the *Collins English Dictionary* as 'the process of bringing a person to an agreed standard of proficiency by practice and instruction'. Training is about passing on information, skills and knowledge. Training helps people to develop cognitive skills and capabilities. It usually, but not always, takes place in groups and can be spread over anything between half a day to several weeks. While often directive – 'do this in that way' – training is also sometimes delivered in a coaching, facilitated style by asking questions. However, that does not make it coaching. The primary difference between the two is that one imparts information and the other draws existing knowledge and understanding out of the person concerned. One advantage of coaching over training is that learning is more likely to be sustainable because the coach works with the client over a period of time until their goal has been achieved. Coaching can also be tailored to meet the precise requirements of the individual.

Consulting

When companies have a problem or want to develop, they sometimes bring in consultants who observe, analyse, probe, offer solutions and show or tell the company how to do something. Once the consultant has explained all the ins and outs, they leave the company to their own devices, sometimes with a 'manual' to refer to if they get stuck. Coaches tend to stay with companies during the implementation phases.

Traditionally, the consultant's role has been as 'expert', but increasingly consultants adopt a client-centred approach that is more like coaching, and they may explicitly offer coaching as well. Instead of telling clients what they should do, many consultants now work by drawing options out, and presenting a range of possible actions.

Counselling

Counsellors, like coaches, create a space in which clients can open up and talk about their issues. The key difference is that counselling deals primarily with helping people overcome problems whereas coaching is concerned with enhancing performance. Counselling tends to focus on the past in its search for reasons why we behave the way we do. The goal is to assist people in understanding the root cause of long-standing issues. Coaching tends to look more to the future. Counsellors often use 'Why?' questions such as 'Why do you keep doing that?' whereas coaches more often ask 'What?' questions such as 'What would you like to do instead?'

Therapy

The purpose of therapy is to deal with a psychological problem such as a phobia, unwanted habit, panic attack, obsession or trauma. This is an interventionist approach in which the therapist uses techniques and processes to resolve issues. Coaching operates on the basis that the client is already functioning well and wants to move on to a higher level of effectiveness.

Types of coaching

Part of the confusion surrounding coaching is due to the fact that there are so many different types. The main ones are listed and explained below:

Life coaching

Life coaches work with members of the public on a wide range of issues. Although coaching is supposedly 'not remedial', in practice many of those who seek it out have issues that they would like to resolve, such as wanting to earn more money or meet their soulmate. In our experience as practising coaches, only a small minority of clients have wonderful lives that they would like to make even better.

Executive coaching

The name says it all – executive coaches are involved in coaching executives and senior managers. Business-related issues are the principal targets, but most coaching works on the basis that everything is part of a system and some 'personal' matters – such as the effect of working long hours on personal relationships – are often addressed as well. The main focus, though, is usually on areas such as leadership, strategy, entrepreneurship, team-building and managing change. More often than not, executive coaches operate externally to the business and have past experience of working at a senior level. A small number of companies employ 'in-house' executive coaches, who work for them full time and are also sometimes involved in training, business development or human resources.

Corporate coaching

Corporate coaching has a wider focus than one person, and deals with the whole of a business. This is typically used with larger companies, and includes coaching teams and relationships within organizations. Consultancy work such as helping to create a coaching culture also falls under this banner. Corporate coaches require in-depth knowledge of organizational culture and an understanding of the systems dynamic – which means they explore the whole system and take a holistic approach to their work.

Business coaching

Business coaches usually work with business owners and managing directors of SMEs (small to medium-sized enterprises) looking to make them more successful. The work involves defining short- and long-term business goals, creating business plans, developing marketing plans and reviewing company processes. Although they are known as coaches, business coaches tend to wear several hats – acting as consultants, mentors and coaches.

Performance coaching

Managers who have responsibility for teams are often required to provide coaching for their staff. Where performance goals and targets are set, coaching skills can be used to help people overcome obstacles that are holding them back and to stretch good performers so they fulfil their potential. The aim is to increase the team's effectiveness and productivity at work. Performance coaching takes place on an everyday basis, not just once or twice a year when it's time for a review.

Specialist coaching

Many life and executive coaches work with a wide range of issues, but some only focus on one or two issues that interest them or in which they have expertise. Mark Forster, author of *Get Everything Done and Still Have Time to Play* (2000), is a specialist coach on Time Management. Arianna Gee, co-author of *Be Your Own Love Coach* (2005), focuses on relationships.

The word 'coach' is also increasingly being used by business people who offer a particular service. Assertiveness trainers style themselves as 'confidence' coaches, and financial advisers present themselves as 'wealth' coaches. There's nothing wrong with this, but it can muddy the waters as far as the public is concerned. Some specialist coaches abide by the principles of coaching, following the client's agenda and asking questions, while others are more directive in their approach.

Career coaching

Career coaching is a specialist area where coaches work with people who wish to improve their job satisfaction, change roles or make a career change. A career coach's aim is to help their client to gain increased clarity over the direction of their working lives. They also help the client to understand themselves better so they can design a career that works for them. Career coaches often use instruments that measure an individual's competence and provide both coach and client with valuable insights into possible career avenues they had not considered before.

Is coaching the right choice?

Coaching is not right for everyone or for every situation. If you suspect a prospective client has psychological problems, then therapy would be more appropriate. And if you have started to work with someone and you discover that their issues seem more deep-rooted than you had thought, suggest that they seek out someone better able to help them. You do not need an in-depth understanding of psycho-dynamics to coach, but you do need to be alert to signals that suggest you should refer your client to a professional therapist.

Common myths about coaching

There are more than a few myths about coaching that can be challenged before we go any further.

Myth: **Coaching is remedial. It's only for under-achievers.**

Reality: While coaching can sometimes help those who are not fulfilling their potential, training often gives better results in these circumstances – especially where people are unclear about what is required of them or lack specific knowledge or skills. Coaching is commonly used to help those who are already doing well to do even better – accelerating their development.

Myth: **It takes a long while before coaching works.**

Reality: Some people have a perception of coaching as being slow and that it takes a long time to achieve results. Nothing could be further from the truth. It's not unusual for clients to take a big step forward in just the first session, and to continue making solid progress in the sessions that follow.

Myth: **Coaching is only for senior managers and high flyers.**

Reality: It is true that many senior managers and high flyers do have coaches but that is mainly because companies increasingly recognize the value of coaching and can afford to pay for it. This does not mean that 'ordinary' people cannot benefit as well. The great thing about coaching is that it works for pretty much everyone.

Myth: **People want advice – not lots of questions.**

Reality: We live in a culture where offering solutions is the standard response when people have issues they are looking to resolve. Yet that does not mean it's what they want or need. When people are exposed to the coaching alternative asking questions instead of giving advice – they discover they have many of the answers already, which allows them to grow in self-confidence.

Myth: **Coaching takes up too much time.**
Reality: You often hear managers say this. And it's true that if you have a large team and you take a formal coaching approach with each person that this can be a substantial commitment. However, many discover that when they do it, the investment soon pays back.

Myth: **The results of coaching cannot be measured.**
Reality: Few studies have been carried out to measure the effectiveness of coaching, but those which have been done convince the most hardened of sceptics. A study of 100 US executives over a four-year period found a 5.45 times return.

What you can do

- Deepen your understanding of the latest thinking on coaching by reading articles in newspapers and magazines.
- Start practising by using a non-directive approach in everyday conversations to get a feel for how it can make a difference.

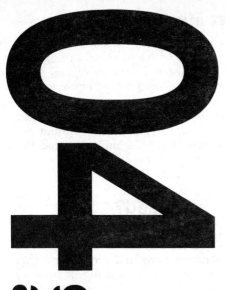

04

getting started as a life coach

In this chapter you will learn:
- about the training you need
- why people hire a life coach
- how to get started
- how much you can expect to earn
- how to find your niche and win clients
- the importance of being able to explain life coaching to others.

Anyone can start life coaching

The great thing about life coaching is that you can just start. It's not like being a dentist or a doctor, where you need a recognized qualification and have to be registered with an official body. There are no barriers to entry whatsoever. All you have to do is say you're 'open for business' and you can begin coaching for money. There's nothing to stop you reading this book, calling yourself a coach and booking your first session – without any training. But we would advise strongly against that and this chapter will explain why.

What training do you need?

Would you want a dentist who'd only done a correspondence course? Of course not. Or a doctor who'd only skimmed through a couple of books on anatomy and physiology. That would be crazy. And it's the same with coaching. It involves other people. Because it's interactive you can't develop the skills just by reading. You need to practise them, and get feedback from someone more experienced, to reach the stage where you are competent to work in a paid capacity.

So if you're serious, go on a course. That way you'll know your skills are up to scratch before you launch yourself upon the general public. People come to coaching with a wide range of issues, and you need to be able not only to deal with them effectively but also know what to do when things get tricky or you feel a little out of your depth. In Chapter 20 we look at what to consider when choosing a coach training programme, so you can feel confident, credible and qualified when you set up in business.

Why people employ a life coach

People employ the services of a life coach for many different reasons. Sometimes they want support in setting goals and seeing them through. Others simply want to explore issues. They may be attracted by a general idea such as 'designing their life' or something more specific, such as:

- **building self-esteem** – many clients seek greater confidence in a variety of situations
- **managing money** – coping with a financial situation that has got out of control

- **making a big change** – dealing with the aftermath of divorce, starting a new business, changing jobs, redundancy
- **handling relationships more effectively** – this can be a spouse, family, friends, a boss or colleagues
- **getting organized** – managing time more effectively and reducing procrastination are topics that often come up
- **knowing what they want from life** – sometimes coaching can be directed at existential issues and working out their life purpose.
- **having more fun** – living the lifestyle of their choice
- **feeling fulfilled at work** – getting the job of their dreams
- **handling conflict** – overcoming interpersonal differences at work or at home, putting a family feud to rest
- **losing weight, getting fit** – making changes so they feel good about their appearance.

Ways of getting started

What exactly does 'getting started' mean? Are you looking for a full-time career as a coach? Or would you prefer to work part-time and supplement your existing income? Are you considering making a clean break, quitting your current job and setting up in business? Or building things slowly, and making the switch only when you're doing enough coaching to feel confident you'll make a go of it. Let's consider the options.

Part-time coaching

Some people like the idea of coaching but don't want to do it full time. Maybe they're happy with what they're doing at the moment, but want more variety. Perhaps they'd like to do something more satisfying, and that's why coaching appeals. Either way, it's perfectly possible to start coaching part-time. Many of the people who come to coaching are in work themselves, and welcome the opportunity to hold sessions in the evening or at weekends.

Building it up slowly

You may be happy doing a few coaching sessions a week, and have no ambitions to go further. But if you fancy becoming a coach full-time you'll ultimately need to make the break from what you're doing at present. You could just hand in your notice, but many people are nervous about diving straight in.

They prefer to put a cautious toe in the water first and manage the transition by doing coaching alongside their existing commitments for a while.

Going part time

If that proves successful, and more coaching is generated than can be accommodated in evenings and weekends, one option is to go part-time at your existing work – perhaps cutting down to three days. This allows you to schedule more sessions – including some during the weekday, which self-employed clients often prefer – and gives you time for marketing as well.

Making the break

This softly, softly graduated approach isn't right for everyone. Some prefer to take a risk and 'go for it'. But it is a risk. It takes a while to build up a coaching business, and you may not be earning enough to pay the bills or put food on the table for some time.

Of course, you may have no choice. If you've been made redundant and are looking for a new direction it makes sense to devote yourself to coaching full time. If you received a reasonable pay-off, this can provide a financial cushion while you get things off the ground – as well as enabling you to fund training, promotion etc. If you don't have any money in the bank you may need to arrange an overdraft or loan to meet your outgoings while establishing your practice.

Amanda worked for a large organization for many years and decided the time had come to go it alone. Her years of employment had allowed her to hone her skills and to get some great experience that was to prove invaluable to her in the future. She had good employers who supported her in the process by allowing her to work part-time while she found her feet with her fledgling business. Her boss at the time commented that he had never seen anyone so sure of what they wanted to do. She gradually built a network of contacts, and offers of work quickly followed. During this time she recognized the importance of continuing to develop her skills as a coach. When Amanda thinks back to this time she still remembers the sense of excitement and adventure from making her own way in the world. She also recalls how valuable that transition period was, without which she would have had very little income to rely on.

For some people there's no 'break' to make. Maybe they're retired, and have income from a pension, so it's not generating money that's driving their interest in coaching. Or perhaps they have a partner who is in a financial position to support them through the often difficult early days.

It's a similar, but different situation, when parents who've stayed at home to look after children return to work. Sometimes they want a brand new start – and coaching is a popular choice. Because there are often issues about picking children up from nursery or school, and problems with doing coaching when they're at home, the best time is during the middle of the day – from 9am to 3pm. Once the practice has been established, the working hours can be extended as the children get older.

How much can you earn?

You can certainly earn money from coaching, but can you make a living from it? Well, it depends what income level you aspire to. The truth is that not many people generate enough from life coaching alone to pay the bills. Many also do training, consulting or have 'passive income streams', from CDs, books etc. which bolster their earnings.

The problem right now is that too many coaches are chasing too little work. That may change in the future, as coaching becomes better known and demand increases. But the volume of people taking training means it's likely to remain a highly competitive field.

A simple 'back of an envelope' calculation will enable you to work out whether it's going to be viable. Tot up all your current outgoings, then add in expenses such as stationery, telephone bills, printer cartridges that you'll incur as a coach, and that's how much you need to earn. Divide it by 48 – the number of weeks most people work in a year – and you have a figure for how much you need to make. Can you realistically do that each and every week? If not you have a problem.

Pricing options

There are many ways you can price your coaching. What people will pay depends on a number of factors, including where you live. How well qualified you are can also make a difference. But getting well known – perhaps by writing a book or appearing on television – can give you a boost and allow you to raise your rates.

Since most clients contract for several sessions, it can be a good idea to get them to commit up-front by charging a monthly fee for a number of months. The actual amount depends upon how many face-to-face sessions there are, how long each lasts, and whether there's any additional support – such as phone or email.

Do a search on the internet under 'life coach' or 'life coaching' and you'll find plenty of sites where coaches detail their prices. Look at a few and you'll get some ideas for how to structure your own rates. You might also want to ring any coaches working in your local area, posing as a prospective client, to find out what they charge.

Finding your niche

When you start out there's a natural temptation to offer coaching on everything under the sun – all the areas we listed above and then some. But that's not necessarily a good idea. That's because prospective clients might think of you as a 'jack of all trades' – and therefore master of none. That's why coaches are increasingly specializing. It's easier to build a reputation when your offering is clear. People often prefer going to someone who's an expert.

So consider whether you want to 'niche' your coaching. You might follow an interest or passion. Or coach on a subject where you have knowledge and experience. This can make you more credible, and increase the volume of business you get – and also the amount you can charge. Paradoxically, the more narrow and specific your target audience becomes the more coaching you're likely to generate because they're clear about what you can do for them – people prefer to go to an expert. It's counter-intuitive to what you think would be the case.

Perhaps you have an interest in families and could specialize in working with parents who want to get on better with their kids. Or maybe you love eating well and going to the gym and would like to coach people on health and fitness. Think about the areas of life you're interested in and how that links to coaching. Some people develop several niches to avoid putting all their eggs in one basket.

Where to find clients

One of the first things you'll need to do is get some clients on your books as soon as you can. Here are some initial ideas (there are lots more in Chapter 19).

- Friends or relatives can be a source of clients – but you should exercise caution here. When you know somebody well that can inhibit you and them from feeling comfortable in a coaching relationship. A better alternative is to ask them if they know anyone who might be interested in being coached.

- Draw up a list of 100 people you know – which could include business contacts – and send them a 'Jane Smart' letter (Jane Smart created a marketing letter specifically for this purpose which is available via the internet to anyone) introducing what you do. You'll find a sample in the Appendix.

- Design a flyer and make enough copies to put through every letterbox within a mile or two of where you live. You can produce one at a reasonable cost on your PC – or get a professional printer to prepare one for relatively little outlay.

- Create a poster or postcard to put up in your local paper shop, library, gym arts centre, health food store, church or Town Hall. In fact anywhere you can think of where people are likely to notice it. Some places don't make a charge for this. And even when they do it's often modest.

- Set up a website, so people can 'find' you when they're looking for a coach on the internet. If you have time and skills you may be able to do something basic yourself, if not it's worth investing in the expertise of a web designer.

Explaining coaching

One thing you'll need to be able to do is explain what coaching is and what its benefits are – quickly and succinctly. Coaching is still in its infancy in the UK – although it's been established in the USA for some years – and not everyone understands what it is and how it benefits others. Tell everyone you meet what you do. Learn half a dozen ways of explaining what a life coach does so it sounds really natural. You might say 'I work with people who want to get clarity over what they want from their life' or if you specialize in a particular area 'I help people take control of their finances'.

What you can do

- Compile a list of people you know who may want to experience life coaching, and ask them if they're interested in trying it out.
- Create a plan of all the activities you're going to undertake to make sure people know about your life coaching service.

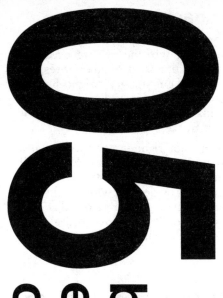

05

becoming an executive coach

In this chapter you will learn:
- about the work an executive coaches does
- how much you can expect to earn as an independent executive coach
- the advantages and disadvantages of working as an external coach
- the part company sponsors play in the coaching relationship
- how to overcome potential obstacles and become an executive coach.

About executive coaching

Many life coaches – and more than a few people in business as well – fancy the idea of breaking into the field of executive coaching. It's an attractive proposition for a number of reasons – not least the money you can make if you get it right. But the work is interesting and stretching too – especially as you move up the levels – assuming you like the idea of working with senior managers and Chief Executive Officers (CEOs).

However, Executive Coaching's not right for everyone. Rates may be much higher, but so are the demands. This chapter will help you decide if you're made of the right 'stuff' and have a desire to do this kind of work. It provides you with insight into the executive coaching world including an idea of what you might earn, typical client issues you'll face, how to deal with company sponsors and obstacles you'll need to overcome if you're to make the grade.

How to break into executive coaching

We need to be honest about this up-front: unless you've had a successful business career, or have experience in consulting or training, it's not exactly easy to break into Executive Coaching. But it can be done. If you're committed to making the move you'll find a way. The easiest point of entry is to look for work with middle or junior managers. Although most people associate coaching in business with working at senior level you need to build a track record first by working with managers 'further down the food chain'.

Companies want coaches to provide individuals with support on a variety of issues including:

- **People management** – the person's behaviour is perhaps abrasive or they are considered to be a poor communicator.
- **Delegation** – many managers resist passing on tasks to others.
- **Enhancing personal impact** – interacting with others in a way that projects and inspires confidence.
- **Dealing with conflict** – sometimes the coach works with both parties individually and then jointly to resolve personality clashes.
- **Planning and organizing** – working with clients who want to streamline the way they handle information.
- **Solving problems** – encouraging analytical thinking.

More often than not senior managers are sent on a course, but from time to time the company decides to 'home in' on a particular issue or behaviour and calls for an executive coach. Coaching outcomes are sometimes linked to competencies used by organizations to assess the level of current behaviours displayed by their managers. Every so often external coaches are employed to support managers with their own career development or help people transition into their next role. Some companies hire coaches to help them handle outplacement of staff during organizational restructuring. Although it's easier to get this type of coaching work you still need to have the right credentials.

Competencies

Many businesses who buy in coaching from external sources are becoming concerned by the lack of regulation in the profession and the fact that anyone can set themself up as an executive coach without experience, training or qualifications. They want some reassurance that the coaches they hire are well-trained and competent to take on the task. The International Coaching Federation (ICF) has developed a set of coaching competencies in an attempt to plug this gap:

- A firm grounding in business knowledge and competencies.
- Thorough understanding of the world of the executive leader.
- A broad understanding of leadership and leadership development.
- Knowledge of systems dynamics.
- Knowledge of the framework of adult development.
- High standards of personal and professional ethics.
- Highly developed communication proficiency allowing the coach to operate in the executive's environment.
- Advanced coaching skills and capabilities.
- Stature and reputation that gains respect.
- A commitment to lifelong learning similar to that of the (client) leader.

What if you don't measure up?

That list can look pretty daunting if you're relatively new to coaching. But don't despair if you can't say 'Yes' to every item. It's still possible to get executive coaching work. The list is something to aspire to rather than a must-have.

Credibility though is essential when it comes to working in business – especially at senior level. Companies often insist upon relevant experience, so if you've never held a management position you may not get taken seriously. If you've worked with different people and in diverse companies that's certainly to the good – and will expand the options available.

If you've only operated in one particular sector, such as banking or pharmaceuticals, you'll probably find it easier to get commissioned to carry out executive coaching in the same area. And if you've been employed in the charity or public sectors, that would be a good place to focus your attention initially. Although it's not impossible to make the switch from public to private, many companies opt for a coach who understands their world and has relevant experience in it. They prefer to go for someone who, at the very least, understands the private sector culture.

This doesn't mean that executive coaches need expertise in the job role of the person they're coaching. If you're coaching an accountant you don't have to understand finance. Nor do you need to be able to come up with innovative new business ideas if you're coaching an entrepreneur.

In fact, if anything, knowledge and experience can get in the way. There can be great value to a client in having a coach who isn't completely imbued with the culture of a company or industry, and who's therefore able to challenge the status quo rather than just accept it. However, companies don't always think like that. Many will only consider coaches who have a background in their industry because they believe time will be wasted by the client having to explain things an insider would already understand.

What companies want

One thing it's useful to understand is that companies often don't make as much of a distinction between coaching and mentoring as the profession does. They expect the coach to do whatever they can to help the person move forward as quickly as possible – including sharing knowledge and expertise where they have it. There's nothing you can do about this. If you don't want to work on this basis – maybe you have a purist view of what coaching entails and don't want to give advice – then you need to make it clear from the beginning. As well as your track record in business, the sectors and companies you've worked for, and the levels you've coached at, those considering buying your services may be interested in the length and depth of your training, whether you have accreditation with a recognized coaching body, and other relevant qualifications. These will not in themselves open the door to executive coaching, but can be useful selling points once the door has been opened. It goes without saying that you also need excellent coaching skills and to embody high personal and professional ethics and standards.

Money matters

When you hear about the rates you can earn doing executive coaching it may sound like a license to print money. But things are not necessarily as they might seem at first sight. You can certainly earn a decent living, but don't set your sights on that expensive sports car just yet.

For one thing, you'll be expected to travel to the client, which could easily be an hour or more each way – and you won't normally be able to charge for that time (though car/rail expenses are normally covered). So it could take you three to four hours to run a one-hour session – which means a rate of £200 an hour effectively becomes £200 for half a day. That's why it's sensible, whenever possible, to arrange longer sessions to make coaching more cost effective.

If you have several clients at one company, the sponsor may be able to organize for them to be coached on the same day – allowing you to run three two-hour sessions at the same location, which works out much better financially. Obviously this isn't a problem with telephone coaching, but at the senior manager level, companies seem to prefer face-to-face sessions – and it may not be an option.

Bear in mind also that few executive coaches are engaged in chargeable work five days a week. They also have to attend meetings with prospective clients, put together proposals and market their services.

Working with company sponsors

One of the major differences between executive coaching and life coaching is that you have two clients. One is the person you're actually coaching and the other is the company sponsor who makes the decision to hire you.

The company sponsor is typically an Human Resources (HR) Manager/Director, Managing Director or other senior manager – tasked with finding a coach for someone. They brief the coach on the company's perspective of the situation before introducing them to the person who wants to be coached.

From the sponsor's point of view coaching can save valuable time away from the workplace when the alternative is sending someone on a course that won't quite meet the person's needs. Many experienced executives have attended every course going already and find much of the content just acts as a refresher – whereas coaching is fast and focused.

It's worth being aware when you're called in to work with an individual who your sponsor thinks has a problem that the boss or company culture can contribute to the problem too. If you ask enough pertinent questions you're likely to uncover the truth. All you need to do then is convince the boss – who is sometimes your sponsor – that they need coaching too or draw their attention to the corporate 'glue' that's getting in the way such as outdated policies/procedures or a company culture that's evolved in a way that holds the organization back.

If the MD calls you in complaining that his team need coaching because they don't use their initiative and leave everything to him and the company has a history of top-down, autocratic style leadership with a procedure in place to cover every eventuality – it's the MD not the team who needs coaching. Sponsors are often too close to the situation to see the wood for the trees.

There are a number of situations that lead to the company sponsor hiring an external coach. They provide coaching for people who have:

- just moved into a high visibility senior post
- taken responsibility for several departments for the first time
- been recruited to a new role that has not been clearly defined
- been earmarked for taking on a senior position
- been moved to another country – expatriates adapting to another culture
- specialist technical expertise and are now moving into management roles

Other reasons for employing external coaches can be where there's rapid company growth and a shortage of talent which means people need to be developed quickly, or in times of rapid organizational change where there's a requirement to embed a new culture. The coach can experience this relationship as a bit of a juggling act – continually attempting to balance the needs of both parties.

Moving up the 'food chain'

Some executive coaches are recruited to provide follow up support for managers who've attended training programmes. Some larger organizations, for instance, run Graduate Development, Talent Management or Leadership Development programmes to groom high potential people and give them a leg up the corporate ladder. They sometimes include coaching and/or mentoring to reinforce the learning and ensure the results are sustainable. While some of this work may be done by in-company coaches it can also be outsourced to external executive coaches.

Working on large programmes like these can present coaches with fascinating and varied work – if you can get it. One of the challenges for the aspiring executive coach is having sufficient experience in related areas. These programmes are often centred round topics such as personal impact, leadership, managing change and customer relationships.

To get this kind of work you must have a solid theoretical understanding of those subjects so you're credible when your client discusses the programme contents with you during the session – not to mention convincing the company sponsor that you're the right person for the job. You absolutely have to keep up to date with the latest theory and practise of core business subjects if you want work like this. Some executive coaches decide to specialize in one area such as leadership or strategy.

Training and consulting experience

If you'd like to become an external business coach, and currently work in a related area such as training or consulting, the most important thing is to get as much coaching practice as possible. You'll already have credibility with potential clients, and the next step is to make them aware that you've extended the range of services you're able to offer. You can also combine your skills and offer the client support with a programme which requires both training or consulting and coaching. It's a great way to build up your experience and clock up some hours of coaching. One of the downsides of this type of work is you tend to spend less time with each individual – sometimes as little as a couple of hours or so per person.

Team coaching

Another string you can add to your bow is team coaching. Rather than coaching just individuals, some coaches work with a whole team at once – much like a football coach does. The Corporate Team Coach gets the team to decide what they want to improve or achieve. Maybe they would like to communicate more effectively with each other or move up a gear to reach an elusive sales target.

The team coach helps them to increase not only each individual's self-awareness but also explores the dynamics of the relationship between team members – all the time aiming to support individuals and the whole group towards attaining their goal.

To be considered and commissioned for this type of work you need to have an in-depth understanding of how teams work. There are plenty of excellent books on the subject, which can help you build up some background knowledge. If you know someone who already does this type of work maybe they'll be willing to let you observe what they do.

Tools of the trade

Many executive coaches are also qualified to use assessment, profiling and/or psychometric tools such as Extended DISC, MBTI and Firo-B. These sometimes form the starting point for either a one-off half day meeting or series of coaching sessions. They nearly all work well with whole teams as well as giving them awareness of why people behave as they do towards others. Some organizations also use 360° feedback to help their managers gain insight into how others see them rather than simply relying on their own self-assessment. This involves the manager asking their subordinates and boss to complete a questionnaire about how they experience the manager's behaviour. If you want to be an executive coach you need to acquire expertise and experience in working with these types of instruments.

What you can expect to earn at this level

Winning large contracts of this type can be extremely lucrative. It also requires quite a lot of effort and typically means writing a proposal. (There's more on this in the chapter on business aspects.) Sometimes you'll be pitching for the business against other experienced coaches. A full day's coaching can mean earning anything between £500 and £2000 per day.

Making it to the top

At the top of the company 'food chain' you'll find Directors, CEOs and Entrepreneurs – and these star performers, like elite athletes invariably have their own coach. But you won't just walk into work like this. You need to have a track record at the highest level, exceptional talent, and a CV to die for.

If you don't have them, forget it – you're kidding yourself. If you've never held down a senior position – at least up to director level – how can you expect to win your client's respect and speak to them as an equal? There are plenty of executive coaches pitching for this work who have run international companies themselves – they've been there, done it, and have experience that can be worth millions to their clients. It's not unusual for coaching at this level to have a strong mentoring element to it, with the executive coach discussing ways in which they've dealt with situations the client is facing in the past. Coaches working with senior people not only have to act as a sounding board but must also be prepared to challenge clients with a strong character – which means they need plenty of confidence in themselves.

What you can earn

When you're coaching at this level it's not uncommon to pick up £3000 a day – or even a percentage of your client's salary. Which means it's possible to make some serious money, but you certainly earn it as it's among the most challenging of all coaching work.

A 'Catch 22' situation

The main problem you have if you want to work with businesses is a classic 'Catch 22' situation. To become an executive coach you need experience, and to get the experience you need to be an executive coach. But 'where there's a will there's often a way'. If you're determined to cut it in the corporate world you'll undoubtedly have some success. However, making it all the way to the top and coaching CEOs may only be possible if you've operated at fairly lofty business heights yourself.

What you can do

- Review the ICF coaching competencies and draw up a list of areas you want to develop.
- Start reading articles in newspapers and magazines on business topics to broaden your understanding of the business world.
- Get yourself on the books of a company that offers executive coaching.
- Decide what level of executive coaching you're aiming for, and then create an action plan for achieving your goal.

06

coaching in companies

In this chapter you will learn:
- what's involved in coaching your own team
- how to recognize and overcome barriers to coaching
- when to call for support and use external or peer coaches
- about mentoring schemes.

Coaching in-company today

In recent years there's been a huge shift in thinking about best practice in leadership and management. The days of command and control are fading into distant memory as companies increasingly embrace the idea of using a coaching style – or even creating a coaching culture. When that happens every manager becomes a coach – right across the board. Coaching becomes an integral part of every line manager's role.

You may be reading this book because you're one of these managers and want to improve your coaching skills. Or you might have been told that you need to, if you're to continue to be effective in your role, or rise to the next level. Perhaps instead you work in-company as a full-time coach – or would like to. Some businesses have people who perform the equivalent role of an executive coaching role internally, although this is often combined with a responsibility for delivering training courses or handling HR issues.

Whatever your reason you'll find some valuable information on how coaching can be considered a management style, learn why it's difficult if not impossible for bosses to coach their teams in the true sense of the word, and gather ideas on how to use coaching skills 'on the fly' – in daily conversations. We'll also be looking briefly at mentoring, which has been around for many years but is currently experiencing a renaissance. It's an increasingly popular way of sharing knowledge and expertise within an organization.

Coaching as a management style

The manager's role has changed tremendously over the last few years. Emphasis is now placed on being able to develop a team rather than just cracking a whip to get a task done. Hay and Mcber (2000) observed the behaviour of thousands of leaders and studied how they motivated people who reported directly to them and came up with six different 'leadership styles' that draw on a full range of emotional competencies.

1 Coercive – demands compliance, 'Do what I say'.
2 Authoritative – motivates people to achieve a vision, 'Come with me'.
3 Affiliate – aims to achieve harmony, 'People are important'.
4 Democratic – seeks consensus, 'What do you think?'

5 Pacesetting – pushes for high standards of performance, 'Do as I do now'.

6 Coaching – developing people for the future, 'What about this?'

Hay and Mcber argued that all styles are useful in certain situations and contexts and that an effective, flexible leader will be able to use each as needed. Daniel Goleman (1998) compares the six styles to a set of golf clubs in a professional's bag. Different shots demand different clubs, and the pro has proficiency with all of them. We each have a natural preference for one or two of the styles, but to be successful as a leader you need to learn the skills and behaviours of the other styles – or you're playing with an incomplete set of clubs.

Surprisingly, the least used style was coaching – even though it was one of the most effective. The physician and writer Manya Arond-Thomas (2004) sums up the benefits nicely: 'The coaching leader helps employees identify their unique strengths and weaknesses and ties them to personal and career aspirations. A coaching approach guarantees that people know what is expected of them, and is a mutual commitment to improve performance.'

Can managers be coaches?

Coaching is, then, an essential style. But one of the reasons it's not as readily implemented as it might be is that it doesn't always sit easily with a management role. As Myles Downey puts it in his book *Effective Coaching* (2001), 'Management and coaching are in some ways incompatible'. What this means is that when you hold a position of power in a manager–subordinate relationship there will always be a conflict of interest. Managers have a say in the rewards their staff get and can influence their future prospects in the company.

For that reason, we don't believe a manager can ever be a coach in the true sense of the word. Their 'client' will rarely, if ever, feel safe enough to open up fully. And that's one of the principle foundations for a successful coaching relationship.

However, managers can – and should – adopt a coaching style and use coaching skills with their staff, encouraging them to come up with their own solutions and think for themselves, rather than having detailed instructions about what to do and how to do it. Delegating and empowering in this way will develop people so they are more able to handle different situations without direction.

Changing hats

Some managers get round this 'incompatibility' by letting their team know clearly when they're 'changing hats' – making it plain when they're using a coaching style and when, for instance, they're monitoring performance. But this still doesn't solve the problem.

How comfortable would you feel about letting your manager know you're having problems or that you don't feel confident in certain areas? Exactly. You'd be happy opening up to an independent, external coach – but to your boss you try to look good. Even if your 'manager coach' promised faithfully to keep confidential anything you said, and not to 'use it against you in evidence', you'd still be sceptical – and rightly so.

The secret is probably to start small and use your coaching skills on a day-to-day basis – as one of your preferred management styles. Over time you'll build trust and people will be more willing to engage in a formal coaching process.

Getting started

In most companies if you want to take a coaching approach with your staff you can 'just do it'. At its simplest it involves asking questions rather than dishing out instructions. You'll come across many opportunities on a daily basis to use your coaching skills with people. We've just picked out a few ideas to get you started:

Someone asks your advice

When one of the team comes to you for advice you have the perfect opportunity to coach. Avoid the temptation to give them your solution. Yes, it's the quickest and easiest way. But it's not the best. Instead, ask them to consider various options with you. People often know the answer already or know where to find it, and just need the confidence they can do it themselves. Use this coaching approach a few times and your staff will start solving their own problems – and won't need to bother you so much in the future which will save you oodles of time down the track.

Sample dialogue

Tina: I'm not quite sure how to go about writing this report.

Manager: What have you considered so far?

Tina: Well I need some kind of introduction, to explain the three options, and then I need to make a recommendation I suppose.

Manager: That sounds good. What else might it be useful to include?

Tina: I was looking at last year's report and thought I could put a section on the scope of the project and a breakdown of costs.

Manager: Anything else?

Tina: No, I think that's probably it.

Manager: Great. I look forward to reading it.

There's a problem and you need to review what went wrong

When there's a problem it's dead easy to wade in and sort it all out. But this makes the team even more reliant on you to provide the answers. So try a coaching approach instead. Ask them how they think it should be handled and continue to ask questions until they find a solution for themselves.

Sample dialogues
Instead of:

Ilesh: We're way behind with compiling the data for this month's mailshot.

Manager: Right. Let me see what's going on. Ilesh you get the information from Marketing. Helen, you start pulling everything together. I'll grab the envelopes and take a look at the letter.

Try:

Ilesh: We're way behind with compiling the data for this month's mailshot.

Manager: What needs to be done?

Ilesh: Helen has been in touch with Marketing to get the brochures and I've approved the letter. It is just a bit 'touch and go' whether we'll make this afternoon's post.

Manager: What options have you considered?

Ilesh: We need to put some pressure on Marketing to be sure they come up with the goods, and I suppose we could work through lunch to make sure it's finished on time.

When something goes right

Coaching isn't just for when things go wrong. You can also use it to capitalize on success, learn from it and repeat it. Taking the time to celebrate when things go well encourages 'more of the same'. You can ask coaching questions to uncover the pattern of events that led to achievement. Often people don't know precisely what they did that was so effective, and it can be useful to help them become aware.

Sample dialogue

Manager: I hear the presentation went well. Great bit of business to get. They're not an easy bunch to deal with. How did you pull it off?

Caitlyn: Maybe it's down to all that research I did upfront, and I suppose I have built a good relationship with James.

Manager: That's good. What specifically did you do?

Caitlyn: Just chatted to him really. He was telling me about all the problems he's having with his son and I started to really get to know him. I suppose he trusts me much more now because he's beginning to recognize that I'm on his side. (Pauses and then laughs) Maybe I should use that approach with Simon – he's a tough nut to crack!

You need to ask for information

As a manager you need to know what's going on. But rather than leaping in feet first notice what's going on around you and then request more information. What are people working on? Where do they need more help? How can you support them? If Meeta has a big client pitch coming up use coaching questions to help him make sure he's covered all the angles.

Sample dialogue

Manager: You don't get a chance like this all that often – let's have a chat and you can tell me how you plan to approach it.

Meeta: Great, thanks. I need all the help I can get right now.

Manager: Based on past experience, my bet is that you've got it covered.

Meeta: Well, we thought we'd start with the fact that they can't afford not to go for it and then throw up some figures that show where their market share will be if they say no ... (Continues to describe the pitch in detail)

| Manager: | What could you do to convince them that we're the best company? |
| Meeta: | I guess we could include some testimonials from other similar clients to show we've done the same kind of work. |

Such coaching conversations often last only a few minutes. If it becomes apparent that more time is needed you could schedule a meeting to discuss things in detail.

Analysing options

If you are coaching your staff, or working as an independent coach in a corporate environment, the Skill/Will matrix can be used to assess a person's ability and willingness to accomplish a given task or goal. It allows you to select the appropriate intervention and agree your approach with your client. It's particularly valuable when deciding how to support your own staff. Skill relates to their capability/knowledge/experience and Will is about the degree of motivation they feel towards completing the goal.

Figure 2 the Skill/Will matrix

High will	Train/Guide	Coach/Delegate
Low will	Direct/Redeploy	Motivate/Excite
	Low skill	High skill

The skill/will matrix is an adaptation by Keity, Goldsmith & Co. Inc. of original work by Hersey and Blanchard, *Management of Organizational Behaviour: Utilizing Human Resources* (1977)

Managers need to determine whether their team members are motivated and willing to learn (high will), or going through the motions (low will). They will know who is new to a role or even in the wrong job for them (low skill) and where their people are competent and experienced (high skill). If there is low skill and high will they need guidance and training to acquire the knowledge and skills to do the job. If there's low skill and low will they're best moved elsewhere or given clear instructions of what to do. If there is high skill and low will the manager needs to create a working environment that motivates them. Where there's high skill and high will coaching is the ideal way of encouraging them to excel – giving them the freedom to do things their way.

Working within a coaching culture

Some companies have already established a coaching culture in which all line managers have basic coaching skills. The climate encourages the use of coaching skills throughout the organization. When an effective coaching culture exists, people welcome feedback at every level and challenge each other constructively. Coaching is considered to be an opportunity to grow rather than remedial. Managers who coach are rewarded for doing it well – and given feedback on how they might improve their skills still further. Senior Executives act as role models and aim to remove any barriers to success.

Working in a business where coaching is valued will support you in developing your skills – in the same way that a seed placed in fertile soil with lots of water and sunshine and fertilizer quickly grows into a mature plant.

Companies wishing to establish a coaching culture often engage the services of organizational development specialists because they need support in bringing about a complete change in approach. This means making sure that individual, team and organizational learning are integrated and what's required from every employee is clearly communicated. If this is starting to happen in your company you can play your part by gaining an understanding of coaching and cascading this to your team.

If there isn't a coaching culture

If there isn't a coaching culture in place you may want to consider how the current climate might inhibit you. If senior management still operate in an autocratic way – primarily using a coercive or pacesetting style which involves telling people what to do – you're likely to find it challenging to begin with.

This doesn't have to mean you can't overcome it and create your own coaching culture – even if it's only in your own patch. All you need to do is to totally immerse yourself in what coaching and learning mean and demonstrate you value them on a daily basis. If you're successful, other departments may well start to follow in your footsteps, and a coaching culture could then develop.

Taking your coaching skills to the next level

If you want to get full value out of your skills you need ultimately to go beyond coaching on an ad hoc basis. This means setting aside time for staff development – which might just be an extension to existing one-to-one meetings. If you do plan to introduce regular 'coaching' sessions, start by letting your team know what you intend. It's important to keep them informed and to allay any concerns they might have.

Deciding who to coach first can be fraught with difficulty. Why those people in particular? Is it because they need help, or because they're doing well? Those are the kinds of questions the team will be asking.

You might be tempted to choose someone you think 'needs' it most – but this can create the impression the coaching is about fixing people who are not performing. Then again, if you pick out your star performers others will feel disillusioned because they're not among the elite few. One shrewd option is to ask for a couple of volunteers, explaining that you want to develop your coaching skills, and are looking for people who wish to enhance their performance. Once you make this clear and they experience what 'coaching' from their manager can be like they'll start to feel a lot more comfortable about it. Over time you can bring more people on board.

Making time for coaching

Finding people to 'coach' may be easy. Making time to 'coach' can be more of a challenge. Even those with a small team can struggle to organize one-to-one sessions with everyone, while those responsible for a large workforce – possibly even working in remote locations – might consider such a suggestion pie in the sky. So you'll need to be realistic.

In a survey by the Center for Coaching and Mentoring (2004), 80 per cent of leaders questioned reported they spent four hours or more per week on coaching. 'If you believe,' said one leader, 'the time becomes available.' In other words, if you consider coaching to be important you'll do it. One way to ensure you prioritize it is to plan ahead. Getting the dates scheduled as you would any meeting is one of the best ways to make it happen.

In the beginning it may be difficult to 'ring-fence' slots in your diary for this, but it gets easier as you go along because your staff will progressively become more self reliant and require less of your time.

What if you can't coach everyone?

If you have a large team of direct reports or your people are based in remote locations, it can be a real challenge and highly impractical to schedule time with everyone straight away. The best way forward is to simply get started. Once you begin to make progress you'll learn what works best for them and for you. If it's easier – especially where some individuals are at a distance – set up half hour telephone 'coaching' sessions instead.

Calling for support

When you work closely with someone it's all too easy to lack objectivity about them and their performance. You need to be able to set aside your ideas about the person and approach the coaching relationship with an open mind. If you can't do this for any reason you may not be the right 'coach' for the person – and you should consider alternatives. This support can come from other managers or in-company coaches and from external sources such as hiring an independent executive coach.

Peer coaching

Some – mainly larger – businesses have set up peer coaching relationships to get round the obstacles faced by most people in business who want to coach in the full sense of the word rather than just using coaching skills. This arrangement allows managers in one department or geographical area to set up a reciprocal arrangement with another part of the business. In smaller companies, or where there are no full-time coaches available in-house, you'll need to consider employing an external coach instead.

External coaches

In smaller companies, or where there are no full-time coaches available in-house, you may need to use an external coach. Although company money is most often only spent on senior management when it comes to coaching, you may be able to argue your case and win the funding. It takes a high level of self-awareness to recognize that a manager may benefit from external coaching, and yet some people only feel truly comfortable talking with someone from outside who is completely objective and has no attachment to anything connected to the company.

Mentoring schemes

Many companies have also established mentoring schemes in which typically a more knowledgeable person, who has been in the company for some time, acts as a guide and role model to someone with less experience. It can be a dynamic relationship in which the long- and short-term needs of both the individual and the organization are met. More often than not mentors are allocated a protégé to work with for a period of time from another part of the business. Most mentors use coaching skills as well as advice when they're working with someone. If you want to develop coaching skills it can be useful to offer your services as a mentor. Such schemes are normally aimed at people with potential to go further in the organization and it gives you the chance to practise your coaching skills with a wide range of potentially bright and stimulating people.

Coaching your boss and colleagues

Coaching skills aren't just useful for developing staff. They can be invaluable when dealing with your boss and colleagues too. Listening carefully to what they say, using questions to gain clarity, and giving feedback can be effective with anyone you work with. If, for instance, you're unsure what your boss wants from you, ask coaching questions until you're crystal clear. Sometimes people aren't sure what they want themselves and welcome some assistance in bringing things into sharper focus.

What you can do
• Schedule a series of coaching appointments with each member of your team.
• Get the team together for a 'Question and Answer' session so they can find out more about coaching.
• Practise coaching at every available opportunity.

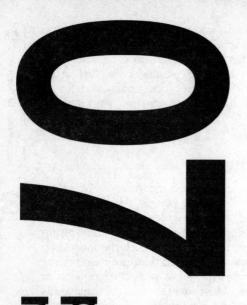

07
practical matters

In this chapter you will learn:
- about the timing of sessions
- how to schedule sessions in a way that works for you and your clients
- when and where to coach.

Getting ready to coach

'Don't agonise, organize'

Florence Kennedy.

Imagine you're about to take on your first coaching client. The telephone rings. You answer and the voice at the end of the line starts to ask you question after question about how coaching works – what they can expect, how much it costs, how long the sessions are and so on. Whether you're a manager who coaches in-company or an external Life or Business Coach you need to have answers to all these questions at your fingertips. As our hypothetical caller's questions reveal, there are a host of practical things every coach needs to consider before they actually start coaching anyone. These include:

- methods of coaching
- where the coaching will take place
- how many sessions
- the duration of sessions
- the gaps between meetings
- scheduling appointments

It's essential to have all that sorted, and be ready to answer a prospective client's questions from the outset. First impressions count. You need to come across as professional and competent. If you sound like you don't know what you're doing you'll struggle to get business. It's important to remember that from the first time you speak with a client they'll begin to get a sense of what it will be like to work with you, and you're starting to build a relationship with them.

Coaching methods

How are you going to do your coaching? The most common approach is face to face, but it's not the only way. Coaching over the telephone is also popular and, thanks to modern technology, other options include video-conferencing, internet 'Messenger' chat – such as MSN, AOL and Yahoo – and email.

Many coaches offer their clients a choice, charging more for face-to-face coaching and less for telephone, video, chat and email options. Some offer 'packages' which combine various elements – often face-to-face or telephone sessions with internet or email support in-between. There are pros and cons to each method.

Telephone coaching

The great advantage of telephone coaching – for both coach and client – is that all the lost time spent travelling to and from the meeting place is eliminated. This means you can fit more sessions into a day and clients don't have to spend so much time away from their work commitments or leisure activities. It also makes it possible to schedule sessions at unsociable times, such as in the evening or at the weekend, without them taking over your life.

And telephone coaching can be every bit as effective as working face-to-face – sometimes more so. Clients can often feel more comfortable about opening up and discussing 'difficult' issues when you're not sitting opposite each other. Not having the visual channel to process means you listen more carefully and hear things you might otherwise miss.

Face-to-face coaching

But not all clients – nor indeed all coaches – like telephone coaching. Many prefer to work face-to-face because it seems more 'natural' and normal to do so. You can see the other person's body language and facial expression, and as a result it's easier to establish and build rapport. However, you do need to be in the same place and that inevitably means one or both of you travelling. This isn't a problem if you live close to each other, but is an issue when there's some distance between you. Ideally you want them to travel to you, so you're not wasting time which isn't chargeable, and that's normally the arrangement with life coaching. But with business clients you will generally be expected to go to them.

Internet coaching

Coaching by means of an internet chat system is slowly but steadily growing in popularity – but is far from being the norm. Like face-to-face and telephone it's interactive and operates in real time – your client types something and once it comes up on your screen you respond immediately. However it's even more impersonal, because you neither see the person nor hear their voice. For that reason it's rarely used on its own – more commonly as an adjunct to face-to-face or telephone sessions.

Email coaching

The problems with internet coaching also apply to email coaching. Because the interchanges are so much more protracted, it's more useful where the client is looking for more advice and guidance. Typically they will sign up for a number of sessions or for an unlimited period at a set fee until they've achieved a specific outcome. After registering they are sent an on-line questionnaire to complete which is used by the coach to shape the first email-based session.

Where to coach?

If you work mainly as a life coach you may be able to work from home. All you need is a room that's smart and clean where you won't be disturbed. The big advantage of this arrangement is that you don't have any overheads. Should you hit a slow, quiet spell where clients are few and far between, you won't have the worry about how you're going to pay the rental on office space. You'll also have the convenience of not having to dash off whenever you have a session. When you're starting out you may only have a handful of sessions spread out through the week at times that suit your clients, and it's a whole lot easier if you only have to step into the next room to run a session.

But working from home may not be possible. You may not have a room that's suitable. You may have noisy neighbours. Or you may have other people in the house. It can be very distracting for both coach and client if there are noises in the background – or worse still that the session gets interrupted mid-flow. Animals sometime create a similar problem. It's hard to concentrate with a dog barking in the distance or a cat scratching at the door.

If for any reason you can't work from home, or prefer not to, you'll need to hire an office or room. What you want if you can get it is a space you can use as and when you need it. There are places that offer this kind of service in most of the major cities, but you may not find it so easy to find somewhere in a rural location. Cost is, of course, an important consideration. The amount you spend hiring a room needs to make sense in relation to the amount you're earning. If you're charging £50 an hour for life coaching and paying £15 an hour for a room, your net rate is only £35 a session. So once you have a decent level of business, it makes economic sense to rent a room or office space on a monthly basis, allowing you to use it whenever you want.

The situation for Business and Executive Coaches is different. The coach will generally go to the client and you may have little or no control over where the session takes place.

Many business people are extremely busy and want to minimize the time spent away from their desk. So, chances are that the coaching will take place in their office, if it's private or, more likely, a meeting room if they work in an open plan environment. On occasions you will meet a client at an outside location, such as a hotel.

Coaching people where they work can often be a challenge. You're likely to be distracted by phones ringing or people knocking on the door – even if you've said you don't want to be disturbed. You also need to make sure your conversation can't be overheard. If confidentiality is an issue your client won't feel able to speak freely.

For all these reasons you should try to get them away from their desk if at all possible – even if it's finding a quiet corner in the reception area of a nearby hotel. One of the advantages of doing this is people tend to relax more in a neutral place which means they feel free to talk openly.

Make the environment conducive

Wherever you coach, it's important to create a conducive environment. The seating needs to be comfortable – but not so comfortable they're likely to fall asleep. You'll also want it to be light and airy if possible, and large enough to use a flip chart or whiteboard if required. Coaches trained in NLP (Neuro-Linguistic Programming) may want to get their clients to have space to do exercises such as perceptual positions.

Think carefully about how the room is arranged, and be prepared to change it if necessary. Avoid sitting across a desk if you can, because that creates a barrier. If you must sit opposite your client make sure there's nothing in-between. The last thing you want is for the session to feel like an interrogation or job interview. Sitting side by side and at a slight angle works well. Your aim should be to create a relaxed but professional atmosphere. Offer your client tea or coffee when they arrive, and have drinking water to hand during the session. You may find it useful to have a clock in the room so you can both keep an eye on the time

How many sessions?

One question that's often asked by prospective clients of a coach is 'How many sessions will I need?' And the answer usually takes the form of two words: 'It depends'. There are so many factors it's generally impossible to say – unless the person has a specific issue they want to deal with, when one or maybe two 'breakthrough' sessions are all that's required.

What commonly happens is that the client will 'contract' for an initial six sessions over an agreed period – often three months – after which the situation is reviewed and a decision made whether more sessions would be beneficial. A coaching relationship can run for years if the client finds it useful, and the coach is happy to continue, but most come to an end within six months.

One factor which affects the number of sessions a client signs up for is money. Few people have an inexhaustible fund of cash, and may only be able to pay for, say, three or six sessions. It's a similar situation when you're acting as an external business or executive coach. The company will almost certainly have allocated a budget for the coaching, and will want to make sure they get plenty of 'bang for their buck'. This can result in them seeking to constrain the number of sessions, especially if the coaching is for a junior to middle level employee. Businesses often work on the premise that the more senior someone is the more likely their performance will have a significant effect on business results.

Frequency and duration of sessions

Coaching sessions can, within reason, be any length as long as the client is comfortable with the arrangement. But while there are no hard and fast rules, life coaches most commonly offer coaching sessions lasting around an hour. This is sufficient time for a reasonably thorough exploration of a 'meaty' issue, but not so long that the discussion is likely to get drawn out simply to fill the time.

Corporate sessions with an executive coach are often longer. Two hours or even half a day are not unusual – and a whole day not unheard of. An ideal arrangement if you're coaching two people from the same organization is to schedule one in the morning and the other in the afternoon. This has the added advantage of cutting down on travelling time and cost. The manager who coaches is more likely to spend anything between 30 minutes and one hour. The key to getting the duration right is to be guided by your client and if there's a company sponsor involve them in the discussion too.

Every coaching session has a natural 'arc' after which the client will feel the discussion has run its course – at least for the time being. This can sometimes happen before the session is scheduled to end. Even so, it's a good idea to draw proceedings to a close. It can be tempting to continue out of a desire to deliver 'value for money' – perhaps by digging into a brand new area – but the client is likely to need time to digest the learning and some of it may be lost if you press ahead just to fill the hour.

On other occasions the natural 'arc' will fall slightly outside the allotted time, so it's good to be flexible. One week you have a slightly shorter session and the next slightly longer. Look out for the big issue that some clients bring up when there's about five minutes left in the session. What you do in this situation is down to your own personal judgement of the person and situation. One option is to leave it to next time, another to extend the session – or somewhere between these two.

The gap between meetings

Many clients are highly motivated to make rapid progress through their coaching in the early stages and don't want too long a gap between sessions. Normally sessions are no more than two or three weeks apart and the coach and clients rarely schedule more often than one meeting a week – a fortnightly frequency is common. While a gap of one month can sometimes work, the more time that's left between sessions the more likely the client will lose momentum – and as a result take longer to achieve their goals.

Scheduling appointments

Whenever possible schedule sessions ahead of time, so they're all in the diary. It's all too easy for coaching to fall into a 'black hole' if it's left to chance – and you need to know where you are.

Some people like to book the same time and day of the week. The good thing about this is they're less likely to forget and miss an appointment. It's also easier for the coach, especially when they have a number of clients and are trying to juggle diary slots. Make sure you leave a gap between sessions to allow for them over-running or people being late. You'll also need time to clear your mind and prepare for the next client. If you set up a diary system in advance with available sessions clearly identified it's much easier to manage the whole process. In fact, if you can dedicate specific days for coaching, rather than have them spread throughout the week, it will help you to stay in a 'coaching state of mind'.

Time is the biggest challenge for managers who coach. The daily pressures of meeting targets and fitting in yet another meeting can make it tempting to postpone, or even worse cancel, coaching sessions. The best way to tackle this is to 'ring-fence' the time you set aside for coaching and honour any arrangements made – otherwise word will soon get around that you are just paying lip-service to it. If you have to move a session make sure you book another time for it straight away.

The timing of a session can influence its effectiveness enormously. Many people are brighter in the morning, so that's a good time to coach. It's not unusual for people to suffer a drop in energy after lunch, when they feel more sluggish – but sometimes you'll have no choice and will need to make sure things don't get lethargic. Evening coaching session are rare for corporate work – they're more typically held during office hours – although some busy executives do opt for breakfast or supper appointments to avoid disrupting the working day. Some life coaching clients may only be able to make evenings or weekends.

What you can do

- Set up a diary system for your coaching appointments, and block out some personal recuperation time each day so that you continue to be in the best possible state.
- Make notes on how a typical course of coaching sessions will work, including cost, suggested duration and length of gaps between sessions.
- Create a personal set of guidelines for where and when you will coach.

08

in the beginning

In this chapter you will learn:
- what to include in the first session
- about the wheel of life or work
- how to define responsibilities in the coaching partnership
- about the line manager's and sponsor's roles
- how to establish the primary focus and set measurable outcomes for the coaching.

The first session

Whatever discussions have gone before, it's during the first session that coaching actually begins. Whether you're life coaching or working in a business environment many of the principles for a good 'intake', 'discovery' or 'contracting' session – the initial meeting can be described in various ways – are broadly the same. There are a number of things to cover if you want to get off to a good start:

- what will happen in the first session?
- the client's experiences and/or expectations of coaching
- establishing your coaching credentials, explaining your approach
- completing a coaching agreement
- issues of confidentiality and trust
- defining responsibilities in the coaching partnership
- accountability
- anticipating setbacks
- getting to know your client
- pre-coaching questionnaire
- using profiling tools
- values elicitation
- the wheel of life or work
- primary focus and establishing measurable outcomes
- deciding whether you're right for each other.

Even if you've already discussed many of the items on the list with your client when you arranged the session, it's a good idea to summarize them in this first 'official' meeting.

There's no right or wrong way of conducting an intake session but the content and sequence outlined below is a tried and tested recipe for success. Before you get going there's one other essential ingredient you need to add to the mix. It may even seem obvious, but it's worth saying nonetheless – if this is your first meeting with the person you need to 'connect' with them as quickly as possible.

Nothing is more important at this early stage in the relationship. You'll be asking them to reveal personal, confidential information – and they will only be able to do so if they feel comfortable with you. This issue is considered in more detail in Chapter 9.

What will happen in the first session?

The important thing to emphasize to your client is that the first session isn't typical of those that follow. It has a particular sequence to it, whereas the others will be less structured. Giving a brief summary of what you plan to cover helps clients anticipate what's to come and know where they are in the process. It can also be useful to manage their expectations about how much coaching will actually take place.

This depends to a large degree on how much time you've allocated to the intake session. If you plan to get stuck into some of your client's issues you'll generally need more than one hour. It depends on how much you feel you need to know about them before you start and whether you've asked them to complete a pre-coaching questionnaire. As a rule of thumb, allow an hour and a half to two hours for a discovery session that includes some coaching.

The client's experiences and/or expectations of coaching

A good place to start is by asking the client about any experiences they've had of coaching and their expectations of it. They may have already told you when you first discussed the matter, but it can be useful to recap. If you haven't asked them already the following are useful questions to ask:

Have you had coaching before?

If yes:

a What kind of experience did you have?
b What approach did the coach take?
c How was it?
d What worked and what didn't?

If no:

a What do you already know about coaching?
b What questions do you have about coaching?

It's good to air any concerns that your client has, answer any queries, and debunk any myths about coaching – to prevent them being the source of any problems.

Establishing your credentials, explaining your approach

You're likely to have explained your approach to coaching before you reach the intake session but it's a good idea to restate it during the first meeting. Don't go on at great length, just give a brief summary. What you want is for the person to feel you're a competent coach, so they have confidence in you. Tell them about your background, training you've undertaken, any qualifications you have, and your experience of coaching.

Completing a coaching agreement

During the first session you need to complete any outstanding financial or scheduling arrangements. If you haven't already done so, agree how much is to be paid and by when, and how many sessions are contracted. Many coaches include this in a written agreement that's often sent to the client in advance of the first meeting. The agreement usually makes it clear what happens if the client cancels a session or turns up late and deals with issues such as confidentiality and how you will work together. A sample Coaching Agreement can be found in the Appendix at the back of this book.

Issues of confidentiality and trust

Confidentiality is easy where your services have been engaged directly by a client – you simply make a commitment to them that you will not tell anyone else what goes on. As long as you honour this your client will trust you; if you're tempted to spill the beans to someone else and your client finds out the trust will be gone. To be trusted you need to be trustworthy.

When you're life coaching it's easy to follow that principle to the letter. When you're working as an executive or business coach, though, and a company is footing the bill, the sponsor or the individual's line manager may expect some feedback. If this is the case discuss it with all parties concerned and establish a process that everyone can buy into. The ideal is for the person you're coaching to take responsibility for what they report back to the sponsor and line manager. One thing that helps is to have some measurable way of establishing progress. This can be verified without details being given of what actually went on in the sessions. Don't gloss over this issue, assuming it will come out in the wash. It won't. You have to agree it up front. If you don't, the client won't feel free to talk openly. It's a similar situation when you're an in-company coach. It's essential your clients feel safe to say anything they want without fear of their line managers finding out and recrimination following.

For managers coaching members of their team the issue is even more complicated, because arguably there can never be confidentiality in what is said because of the relationship that exists.

Many coaches find it invaluable to be able to discuss their coaching with another – often more experienced – coach, who acts as a supervisor. If this is the case the coach may choose to discuss some specific details of the session if necessary. Most clients are happy with the idea of coaching supervision providing the role of the supervisor is explained to them. The supervisor is, of course, bound by the same confidentiality agreement.

Defining responsibilities in the coaching partnership

It's important to agree with your client how you're going to work together in partnership if you are to make the coaching a success. This is often called 'Creating the Coaching Relationship', and in the Co-active Coaching model it's called 'Designing the Alliance'. The term 'designed' reflects the fact that it's tailored to suit the client. It's an 'alliance' because both coach and client are responsible for making it work. But it's the client who's really in charge. They define the direction the relationship takes and are responsible for making sure the coach is supporting them in the best way possible. This doesn't mean the coach won't challenge or say things the client finds difficult to hear – quite the opposite. What it does mean is the client is an equal partner in making the relationship a successful one.

You don't just 'design the alliance' and stick with it all the way through. The process is fluid and the design changes as the relationship develops. The great thing about working in this way is that it starts with the end in mind. When the coaching is over the client will need to be able to fly solo. If they become too dependent on the coach during the relationship they'll find it hard to let go.

For you to play your part you need to be clear about what kind of coach you're going to be. Ask your clients how they like to be coached and decide how you'll work together. Some clients, for example, talk at length and love to give a detailed description of who said what. When you've only got an hour together your time is precious. While you'll be interested in their story you want to make sure best use is made of the time, and that means you'll interrupt them. Interrupting is covered in more detail in Chapter 15.

You may also want to explain that you won't be waving a magic wand but will be there to support them. You need to be versatile and flexible, adapting your style to the needs of your clients. Make it clear though that if what they need goes beyond what you can do, or want to, then you won't do it. Because many people are unclear about what a coach does, they often ask them for help in areas that are better suited to a counsellor, therapist or some other qualified expert.

Accountability

During the coaching sessions clients will often say they're going to do certain things, such as write the synopsis of a book or spend five minutes a day meditating, and it's important to agree with them during the intake session how they will be accountable for these commitments. It may be that in the following session you simply 'check in with them' to see how they got on. Or they may want you to question and challenge them if they haven't done what they said they would. Accountability is useful because it encourages clients to follow through. They often don't want to say at the next session they haven't done their 'homework,' but what's ultimately important is that clients learn to do things because they want to, not because they feel pressured to. The importance of accountability is examined in detail in Chapter 15.

Anticipating setbacks

If achieving what we want in life was always easy no one would need a coach. If you already knew how to attain a goal you'd have got there by now. But life – and coaching – isn't like that. Coaching often starts off well, with the client making great progress during the first two or three sessions with the client reporting back on all the great successes they've had. Then they either attempt something that doesn't quite work out as planned or progress starts to slow down, with the client occasionally getting stuck. It's important to let clients know during your first meeting that this often happens, so they take it in their stride when it does – rather than worrying that 'something has gone wrong'. There's more on how to handle things in 'When the going gets tough' in Chapter 16.

Getting to know your client

By this stage in the proceedings you will have started to get a sense of what kind of person you'll be coaching. Without being judgemental, just start 'noticing what you notice'. A picture will begin to emerge. Do they seem introverted or extroverted? Are their thoughts organized and clear, or scattered and fuzzy? Do they use visual, auditory or feeling language? The more you understand your clients – their aspirations, what makes them tick, their concerns, what their dreams are – the more effectively you'll be able to offer support throughout the coaching relationship.

Pre-coaching questionnaire

One of the best ways of hitting the ground running is to ask your client to complete a pre-coaching questionnaire and return it before the first session. This can include almost anything you find useful – but don't make it too long or complicated. Here are some of the things you might include:

- Name.
- Contact details such as phone numbers, email and addresses.
- Background information including occupation, job title and date of birth.
- A brief CV or elements of it where this is relevant.
- What specific outcomes do you want from the coaching?
- What is important to you?
- What drives you mad?
- List your abilities and qualities.
- Where do you feel most stuck?
- What would you like to change?
- What would you do with your life if earning money were no object?

Many clients comment on how such questionnaires made them think quite deeply about their issues before the coaching has started. Some coaches work through the questionnaire with their client, others dip into it when appropriate, for instance, referring to the client's primary focus. We recommend the latter method because it allows other issues to emerge while completing values elicitation or the 'wheel of life'. In the Appendix you'll find a sample questionnaire you can adapt to meet your own requirements and preferences.

Using profiling tools

Some coaches are experienced and trained in using psychological profiling tools, such as the Myers-Briggs Type Indicator (MBTI) or Extended DISC (Dominance, Influence, Submission, Compliance), and use them in their coaching. Business, executive and in-company coaches will also often use 360° feedback questionnaires as part of the coaching process. Whatever tool is used, it can be valuable to ask your clients to complete a questionnaire like this before the first session – so the information is available for discussion.

Values elicitation

One of your aims as a coach is to support people in making the changes they want. And one of the best ways of doing that is to help them become aware of what's important to them – of what their values are. Tony Robbins, author of best selling books such as *Unlimited Power* (1996) and *Awaken the Giant Within* (1992), describes values as 'belief systems about what's right and wrong, good and bad', which is why they're so powerful and important. They can also be elusive, because much of the time they operate 'in the background', out of conscious awareness. But once they've been revealed they can be used as a personal compass that provides direction when making decisions.

How do you elicit someone's values? Simply by asking them 'What's important to you?'. The list they come up with will typically include both specifics, such as my children and my job, and abstract concepts, such as integrity, making a difference and freedom. It's these 'higher level' values that are most valuable to the coach, because they represent what's most important to the person. If your client only gives you specifics, you can go to the next level by asking questions such as 'Why is this important to you?' or 'What does that give you?'

Example

Client: I'd say my job is one of the things I value most.

Coach: What does that give you?

Client: (Laughs) Well I earn lots of money!

Coach: (Laughs too) And what's important about lots of money?

Client: (Reflects for a moment) I guess it's the freedom it gives me.

Coach: So you value freedom.

Client: Yes, I guess I do.

You can also elicit values by asking people 'What drives you crazy?' and reversing the response. Sometimes we don't even realize we value something until we encounter someone who acts in a way that contradicts or challenges it.

Example

Coach: What kinds of things drive you crazy?

Client: Well, one of my pet hates is when people are late for meetings and appointments.

Coach: Why does that bother you?

Client: Because it's inconsiderate – they just don't respect other people.

Coach: So being considerate and having respect are important values for you.

Client: Very much so.

It's also possible to elicit your client's values by including a form in your Pre-coaching Questionnaire. You can then use this as the basis for a more thorough discussion as part of the intake session. In the Appendix you'll find a template document that contains a more detailed way of not only eliciting values but also defining and prioritizing them.

Leveraging values

When you're coaching someone it's useful to explore the degree to which they're living their values on a day-to-day basis.

Example

Client: You know that interview I went for? Well, they offered me the job.

Coach: Well done. What are you going to do?

Client: I suppose I'll take it. It's a big step up.

Coach: I seem to recall you saying it will involve you spending a lot more time in the office.

Client: That's the only downside. At the moment I'm out three, sometimes four days a week – which I love. If I take the job I'll be tied to the desk most of the time.

Coach: We've talked a lot about how you really value freedom – how would this move fit with that?

Client: That's a good question. After a couple of months I'll probably feel like an animal trapped in a cage. (Pauses) Maybe I should think again.

The Wheel of Life

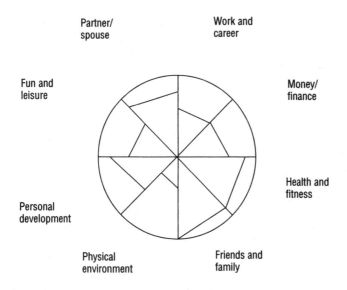

figure 3 The wheel of life

If they haven't done so in the pre-coaching questionnaire, you might want your client to fill-in a Wheel of Life during your intake session (see Figure 3). One of most commonly used tools in coaching – but still excellent even if it's become almost a cliché – the Wheel allows you to get right to the heart of a person's life in a matter of minutes. It's a 'cake' that represents your client's life cut into eight 'slices'. These are typically:

1 Physical environment.
2 Personal and professional development.
3 Money/finance.
4 Family and friends.
5 Partner/spouse.
6 Fun and leisure.
7 Work and career.
8 Health and fitness.

However, these categories are not fixed in stone. You can work with your client if necessary to adapt them to reflect what's important in their life.

The centre of the wheel is 0 and the outer edge of the circle is 10. By marking a line across each segment your client indicates how satisfied they currently are with that area of their life. 10 is extremely satisfied; 0 not satisfied at all. It's important to explain to your client that the wheel isn't who they *are*. It's just a snapshot of where they are at a moment in time – a week or a month later things will seem different. The great value of the wheel is that it gives a perspective on the whole of the person's life at once – which aspects are in balance and which are not.

Physical environment

This segment is devoted to what the client thinks of the place where they spend their time – normally where they live and work. Do they like it? Is it attractive or ugly? Small or spacious? Do they have neighbours that make a lot of noise or are they as quiet as a mouse? How people feel about their home or office space can have a profound effect on their quality of life in general. Small improvements, such as clearing out clutter or painting the walls, can sometimes increase significantly the satisfaction people feel about this segment.

Personal/professional development and spiritual growth

Many people theses days are interested in personal development, as the enormous sales of 'Mind, Body Spirit' books and the growth of coaching itself bear testimony. This is a segment where many clients are looking for a '10' – but that can mean different things to different people. Some want to become more self-aware, to meditate regularly, others more 'enlightened', and coaching the 'spirit' or the 'soul' is very different from helping people learn a new practical skill. There are, of course, lots of ways for people to grow and some clients focus entirely on professional development – wanting to read more books, attend courses, or obtain a qualification. Some people prefer to break this segment down into two or three parts so they can explore how satisfied they are in each area of development.

Money/finance

How much money do you have/earn? What's the state of your finances? Is your income rising steadily or going down the pan? Many clients have money issues they're looking to resolve through coaching. This part of the 'Wheel' is closely connected to some of the others – the kind of work we do affects the money we earn and the time we have to spend with our loved ones and doing all the things we enjoy.

Family and friends

This segment is about close relationships, from children, mothers, fathers, sisters, brothers to cousins, nieces, uncles, nephews and aunts to close friends and sometimes even acquaintances. For many people it's the most important area of their life. Some clients like to split it down to individual people or different groups and give a different satisfaction rating to each of them. They may be happy with their relationship with some family members and in conflict with others, or feel they're not spending enough time with their friends.

Partner/spouse

How someone feels about their closest relationship – or the lack of it in some cases – can profoundly affect every area of their life, from the way they perform at work to their sense of identity. Some coaches specialize in this area alone but most life coaches find they have to deal with issues of this kind on a regular basis as part of general sessions. Some people say they don't have enough time for a relationship but would like one –

the other segments are taking over and leaving no space for someone to come into their life – while those in a relationship range in satisfaction from deeply unhappy to feeling tremendously supported and loved.

Fun and leisure

'All work and no play makes Jack a dull boy' – but often clients find that work and other commitments, such as picking up children and keeping the house clean, squeeze the fun out of the toothpaste tube of life. Leisure can be anything from reading a book to running a marathon to going on holiday – anything that constitutes the lighter side of life. Some clients will be looking to have fun threaded through every segment rather than as a separate category.

Work and career

Executive, business and career coaches focus mainly on this segment, but it figures strongly in life coaching as well. Many people are unhappy in their current job and are looking to change, while others want to develop and hone the skills that will enable them to climb the corporate ladder. You'll also have clients who are working long hours – which has an effect on the health, fun, and partner segments. In fact, work/life balance is one of the most common coaching issues in both personal and corporate work.

Health and fitness

Many people are unhappy with their health and fitness, and it's not unusual to see low satisfaction ratings in this segment. Sometimes it's the reason they seek coaching in the first place. For a host of reasons, including sedentary lifestyles and poor diet, clients can be overweight and unfit – yet only pay lip service when it comes to doing something about it. Visit a gym just after New Year and then again in summer and you'll see how good intentions can vanish into the ether. Yet, surprisingly, some people who are fit and eat healthily – giving themselves a rating of 8 or 9 – are still dissatisfied with this part of the 'Wheel', wanting to achieve yet more.

Working with the Wheel

Once your client has completed the 'Wheel' you can start to explore it together in a spirit of curiosity. Start by asking open questions, such as 'What did you notice when doing the Wheel?' This allows them to discuss the various elements of their life without direction or suggestion from you. Resist the temptation to bring your own perspective into the process – even if the client asks you directly. Encourage them to consider the relationship between the eight segments, and the gap between their satisfaction rating and where they would like to be. Here are some other suggested questions:

- Which segments are you happy with?
- Which would you most like to improve right now?
- What is the relationship between segment X and segment Y?
- What steps could you take to correct the balance?

You can spend quite a long time exploring the Wheel – and it's generally time well spent; if your schedule allows let the discussion run its natural course rather than cut it short. A sample document to use with your clients for the 'Wheel of Life' can be found in the Appendix.

The Wheel of Work

Although at first glance it might seem to be only appropriate for life coaching, the Wheel of Life is sometimes employed by business coaches as well. People's work and personal lives are now inextricably entwined, and using the 'Wheel' means the whole system is considered.

Some Human Resource (HR) Departments, however, don't consider the Wheel of Life appropriate for corporate coaching – and some managers and executives as well. They argue that the focus should be exclusively on work issues and not what happens outside – that the Partner/Family/Health/Fun etc. segments should not be included.

We believe that all coaching should be 'whole-life' coaching, that personal issues can affect business performance – adversely and positively – and vice-versa. For that reason it's not holistic, or effective, to consider one area on its own – they are both part of the same system.

Present that argument confidently and congruently and you will persuade some doubting sponsors and clients. But not all. Another option, therefore, is the Wheel of Work, which can be used to explore the various elements of their business life – such as time management, leadership, delegation and teamwork. You can either suggest the eight segments or coach the client to come up with their own.

In the example shown, a team leader has annotated the wheel with labels relating to areas they consider important and rated their satisfaction with each. Asking similar questions to those for the Wheel of Life will stimulate a useful discussion. Samples of both types of Wheel can be found in the Appendix.

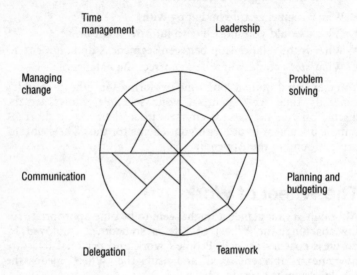

Time management
Leadership
Managing change
Problem solving
Communication
Planning and budgeting
Delegation
Teamwork

figure 4 The wheel of work

Primary focus

Most people come to coaching with one or more issue they want to work on – such as being more confident, getting a better job or avoiding procrastination. It's the coach's role to work with the client – normally during the first session – to clarify what these issues are. The aim is to produce a list of items – it can be as few as one or as many as four or even five – that will form the 'primary focus' of the coaching.

Writing the issues down can provide a valuable reference during later sessions, making it possible to look back on what has been achieved and what's outstanding. As items are discussed and resolved, so they can be crossed off. But it's not unusual for items to be added during later sessions. Sometimes you'll find yourself juggling several issues at the same time with clients jumping back and forth between them. Some people progress quickly from one topic to another, while others spend quite a long time on one issue. And it's not unusual to find the 'presenting issue' getting peeled away, like the layers of an onion, to reveal a deeper concern underneath.

Depending upon the amount of time allowed for the intake session you may have an opportunity to start to work on one of the primary focus issues once you've done everything else. In any case, the mere process of discussing them will mean your clients start thinking deeply about them.

When people have been coached before

When clients have been coached a lot they can easily get into a 'done it before' mode – and be reluctant to fill in 'yet another' Pre-coaching Questionnaire, Wheel of Life or Values Elicitation Form. That can be a challenge for the coach, especially if they're relatively inexperienced, but it's important that you know enough about the client to be able to coach them effectively. However, you won't get far if the person you're working with is putting up resistance, and you'll almost certainly achieve more by getting stuck into the coaching and allowing the information you need to emerge during the conversation.

Deciding whether you're right for each other

At the end of the first session – and even part way through if you sense there are problems – it's a good idea to take stock. Is the coaching what the client expected? Are there any issues that need to be discussed? Is your approach working for them? Both coach and client need to assess whether there's a good fit between their personalities and whether the style of coaching works for the client.

Sometimes clients discover, for instance, that although they supposedly understood your coaching was largely non-directive, they suddenly realize you're not going to give them all the answers to their problems. It may be that what they really need is a mentor. If for any reason the coach and client decide to go their separate ways the coach can always refer the client to someone else.

What you can do

- Create your own pre-coaching pack including:
  - What is coaching?
  - Your approach to coaching?
  - Pre-coaching questionnaire
  - Values elicitation process
  - Wheel of Life and/or Wheel of Work.
- Prepare your own coaching agreement.
- Become familiar with the values elicitation process by completing it yourself or asking a friend to do it.
- Complete your own Wheel of Life and explore the patterns it reveals about your life.

09 connecting with your client

In this chapter you will learn:
- how to create and maintain rapport with your clients
- ways to connect with clients using your voice, sensory language and body language
- how beliefs and values deepen rapport
- about the importance of trust and respect
- about empathy and emotional rapport.

Ways of connecting

Good coaches are experts at connecting. They're easy to talk to, have engaging personalities, and people just naturally open up to them. But when you're starting out you don't necessarily have the confidence or experience to connect with someone you've just met for the first time. And if you have a slightly reserved, shy nature, it can take a while to come out of your shell and get to know them. But there are practical things which speed up the connection – like going from an old-fashioned internet dial-up to broadband – such as:

- voice quality – tone, pace, volume, etc.
- words and the language we use
- body language and gestures
- similar appearance, clothes, etc.
- shared values and beliefs
- mutual trust and respect
- empathy and emotion
- being present.

We'll be looking at these areas and considering ways you can use them to enhance your coaching communication.

The importance of rapport

One of the main ingredients of connection is rapport – as Robert Dilts and Judith DeLozier state, in their *Encyclopedia of Systemic Neuro-Linguistic Programming and NLP New Coding* 'the establishment of trust, harmony and co-operation in a relationship'. In fact, that's a pretty good description of what you need for successful coaching.

Rapport is something that occurs naturally. You only need to reflect on your own relationships to know that, or watch two people having a meal in a restaurant together. They often look like synchronized swimmers. When one leans forward the other does the same. When one takes a drink the other follows shortly afterwards. There's a rhythm to the way they look at each other, how they talk, and when they do things.

Most people don't 'try' to be in rapport with others. It just happens – unless they're trainee coaches out practising their skills! We're completely unaware of the social 'dance' that goes on between us because it's behaviour we learnt unconsciously by observing and copying others as we grew up.

Sometimes we go to a special effort to connect with people – such as when asking for a date or attending an interview. Then we actively, consciously try to find ways of building rapport. Perhaps we smile more, 'turn on the charm', or let them know we have common interests. But most of the time we just 'do what we do' without thinking about it.

You know when people are in rapport because they look comfortable and relaxed in each other's company. They chat easily, laugh a lot and generally get along. You can also tell when people aren't in rapport. They seem awkward and uncomfortable. The conversation sounds stilted and disjointed.

Speeding up the connection

But the fact that rapport is 'natural' doesn't mean it can't be learnt. Speaking is 'natural', but we can still improve the way we do it. The same is true of walking and breathing.

Quite simple things can make a big difference when it comes to enhancing rapport. And because, as a coach, you want to be effective for your client, you'll have the clear intention of establishing a connection with them as soon as possible, and deepening it as the relationship progresses. The client, for their part, will also want things to work, and more often than not will make a conscious effort to get on with you.

It's important, though, to avoid being manipulative when you're attempting to build rapport – perhaps by trying to flatter your client in the hope that they will like you. Compliments need to be genuine and sincere if they're to have any value. What we're talking about are techniques that are mutually beneficial. They allow you to hit the ground running and allow you to support your client in making the changes they want even more quickly.

Building rapport with your voice

Your voice is one of your primary communication tools when you're coaching, so it's crucial that you pay attention to how you use it. You connect with others not only by means of the words you say but also by the way you say them

Everyone's voice is unique – and like a carefully tuned instrument each has its own distinct blend of rhythm, tempo, volume and tonality. Some people speak slowly and carefully, and their voice can be soft and rich. Others blurt their words at

90 miles an hour, barely pausing for breath, at a much higher pitch. There are melodic voices, which have a light, musical quality to them – and are enjoyable to listen to – and monotones, with everything uttered on a single note, which can send you to sleep if you're not careful.

The voice is particularly important in telephone coaching because it's your only channel of communication. And people detect much more than you might imagine – such as an unguarded sigh before asking a question or a change in tone at an unexpected response.

But is your voice working for you? When people first learn to coach they sometimes acquire a 'coaching voice'. It tends to be soft, empathic and understanding – and how many people believe a professional working in the field of personal development should speak. They may not even be aware they've starting talking in a different way. For some clients this will build rapport. The coach will come across as caring and supportive. But for others – particularly business clients – it will be a real turn-off. They might even experience it as false or even patronizing – making it a barrier to rapport rather than a building block.

The first step to building rapport with someone using our voice is by noticing how they use theirs. Are they fast or slow? Smooth or staccato? Deep or high? Musical or monotone? Then all you have to do is match it as closely as possible. That's what happens when people are naturally in rapport.

So doing the same in a coaching session – or a conversation – will increase the feeling of connection. It couldn't be easier. If your client speaks slowly you speak slowly. If they speak fast, so do you. It's the same with rhythm, tone and melody.

Matching is meant to be subtle. If you take it too far you'll sound as if you're mimicking them. So take it steady when you're learning the skill. You'll soon be able to match another person's voice in a sensitive way.

The secret is to practise in a safe environment – such as speaking to a stranger on the phone or buying something from a shop you'll never go back to. Listen carefully, and then copy as closely as you can. If you get it wrong you might get a strange look, but it won't be the end of the world. After a few days you'll be able to match other people effortlessly and easily.

Building rapport through language

Another channel of communication in which you can rapidly build rapport is language. You may have heard/read that there are three main kinds of people – visual, auditory and kinaesthetic – who think mainly in pictures, sounds and feelings respectively. This is true whether they're remembering something, processing reality right now or thinking about the future. And research has shown that the language they use reflects the way they think. A person who's primarily Visual (we use all three senses to some degree) will use mainly 'Seeing' words. Auditory types incline to the use of 'Hearing' language and Kinaesthetic individuals will predominantly use 'Feeling' expressions.

Seeing (visual) words and phrases

Appear, bright, clarity, clear, dark, focus, gaze, glance, hazy, hindsight, illuminate, illustrate, image, imagine, in light of, in view of, look, look into it, mind's eye, notice, observe, opaque, outlook, perspective, picture, reveal, see, short-sighted, spectacle, spot, take a dim view, tunnel vision, vision.

Hearing (auditory) words and phrases

Audible, call, clear as a bell, discuss, earful, earshot, express, harmony, hear, listen, loud and clear, manner of speaking, mention, note, outspoken, remark, say, scream, shout, silence, sing, sound, speak, speechless, tell the truth, tongue-tied, tune-in, voice, wavelength, well informed.

Feeling (kinaesthetic) words and phrases

Affect, bear, bring, carry, cold, crash, crawl, emotion, foundation, get a load of this, get in touch, grab, grasp the nettle, grip, handle, hang in there, hassle, heated, hold, hot-headed, impact, irritate, lukewarm, motion, muddled, press, rub, sharp, shock, solid, stress, strike, tap, throw, tied up, touch.

One way you can build rapport with a client is to use the same type of language as they do. They'll feel an immediate connection that's extremely powerful. If you use different sensory language, it may seem to them that you're speaking in a foreign tongue. How many different sensory words can you identify in this exchange?

Sample dialogue

Client: I just can't handle it and don't understand what she's getting at. I feel really uncomfortable when she's around.

Coach: I can see your point of view but what do you think her perspective might be?

What did you think of the coach's response? The client used mainly 'feeling' words but the coach's reply contains lots of 'seeing' words. A better response would have been:

Coach: I sense this is churning you up inside. How do you think she's feeling about things?

If you're unsure about what sense to use when you've only just met your client use all three. But after a few minutes' careful listening, you'll know which they prefer. There are other clues you can listen out for. When people speak quickly they often have a preference for the visual sense, the slower the voice the more likely it is that the person prefers feelings. Those with an auditory preference lie somewhere in-between.

Repeating back the client's words and phrases

We all have favourite words or phrases that represent how we actually think about things. Don't paraphrase your clients. Whenever possible, repeat back to them exactly what they said. This is another way of connecting with someone. If you use the exact same words as them they'll feel listened to, understood and the rapport between you will deepen.

Sample dialogues
Good example
Client: I've got a new member of staff who's driving me crazy.
Coach: How are they driving you crazy?

Bad example
Client: I've got a new member of staff who's driving me crazy.
Coach: What are they doing to upset you?

Building rapport using body language

People automatically, intuitively match the posture, gestures, and facial expressions of another person when they're in rapport. One leans forward conspiratorially to chat with a colleague. Their workmate follows suit. From a distance they look like identical 'bookends' – mirror opposites. After a while they both sit back, relaxing and smiling over their shared 'secret'.

An easy way to build rapport when you're coaching is to match the position of the client's body and how they move it. If their legs are crossed, then cross yours. If they're open, keep yours open. If their hands are still, keep yours still. If they're moving, then move yours. And so on.

Take care though, that you don't make your movements too obvious. Leave a gap after someone makes a change and you follow suit. Another, more subtle way, is to use 'cross-over mirroring' which involves matching part of the others person's body with a different part of yours – such as, nodding your head in time with their tapping foot. This may seem an unlikely way of building rapport, but trust us – it really does work.

The only way to become a master at using your body to build rapport is to be observant and practise – once again in a safe environment. Take every opportunity to have a go at doing this where you can – perhaps choose someone you meet on a train journey, or when you're out chatting with a friend.

Eye contact

How much eye contact should you make with your clients? This is a difficult question. As in any other social interaction, too much eye contact can be experienced as intimidating, and too little as not being interested. Having periods where you have eye-to-eye contact will help to deepen rapport but keep them brief – just a few seconds at most. Be attentive, but don't overdo it. Let the client know you are present and engaged.

Dressing the part

People who get along and 'hang out' together often dress the same way. You'll see groups of teenagers with an identical style while most city types wear a suit to the office. The way we dress is one of the ways we express our identity. Choice of clothing both reflects and creates rapport.

What does that mean for how you dress in relation to your clients? Well, if you want to build rapport – and you do – you'll need to look broadly the same as them,

If the people you coach are professionals that means smart business attire – perhaps even a tie if you're a man. Turn up to an executive coaching session in jeans and a T-shirt and you may get shown the door. But if you're a life coach, and people turn up casually dressed and you're wearing a suit, they may think you're a bit stuffy and formal, and feel slightly uncomfortable.

Either way it's likely to be counter-productive. So think carefully about what you put on. Don't wear the same thing for every session. Try to match your clients while still dressing in a way that reflects your sense of who you are.

Deepening rapport with shared values and beliefs

But there's more to rapport than similarities, body language and voice matching. The deepest connection between people occurs when their beliefs and values coincide, creating a close bond that's based around empathy and trust. This allows clients to feel safe and open up.

People of the same age, background and culture usually have a lot in common. It's the 'glue' which holds many communities together. So, when you have a client who's like you in one or more of these ways you'll probably experience an immediate sense of connection. You may 'hit it off' together and 'get along like a house on fire'. It's easy to coach someone when you share the same belief and value system.

But what happens when your client is different from you, and there's not that instant rapport? Do you just give up and go home? No, of course not. People come in all shapes, ages, sizes, races and characters. We live in a wonderful world of wide-ranging diversity. And your clients will reflect that. As a coach you'll have an open mind about people. You may not have the same views as them but as long as you accept them as they are, you'll be able to establish, maintain and deepen rapport.

Building rapport with trust and respect

Where there is trust between people, there is tremendous strength.

Pam Richardson, *The Life Coach*, Hamlyn.

Your clients will trust you if you are trustworthy. This means your behaviour matches your values and sense of who you are. For some people this can be expressed in one word – integrity. You say what you do and do what you say. Honesty is also an important ingredient. But there's more to trustworthiness than meets the eye. Many people need to feel respected before they can give their trust. That means having regard and esteem for them no matter what they've done, who they are and where they're going. Mutual respect is the foundation stone of trust in any relationship, and that certainly includes coaching.

You're more likely to win someone's trust if you're prepared to reveal something about yourself. This doesn't mean blurting out more than the other person really wants to know. A little can go a long way. When you reveal who you really are you allow your client to do the same. By showing your vulnerability you allow them to be vulnerable too.

Empathy and emotional rapport

When someone's happy you can hear it in their voice and see it in their expression. When they're sad, angry, fearful, joyful or relaxed it's just the same. As you listen to your clients speaking and observe their body language you're aware of the emotional undertone. If you couldn't hear the words they were saying you'd still know. But how should you respond? Do you match it? Do you ignore it? What do you do to establish emotional rapport? The answer is empathy.

The *Collins English Dictionary* defines it as 'the power of understanding and imaginatively entering into another person's feelings.' When you have empathy with someone you're able to put yourself in their shoes and imagine what it's like to be them. When you, as coach, do that in respect of your client you deepen the rapport you have with them. You experience the world as they do and that inevitably strengthens the connection between you. They feel you're on their wavelength and understand their point of view.

However, it's not appropriate to match your client's emotions too closely. If they come in crying it's not going to help if you start 'blubbing' as well. You need to stay resourceful.

Empathy comes easily to many who are drawn to coaching – it's something they do naturally. There's a difference, though, between empathy and sympathy, which is when you share someone else's emotions. Clients sometimes pour their heart out and are full of tales of woe. If you get drawn into being sympathetic – 'He did what? Poor you!' – you'll only reinforce their sense of being hard done by. When you respond with empathy – 'I can tell you're upset by this' – you acknowledge their feelings but don't buy into them. Continuing with 'What do you think is going on here?' maintains a coaching framework. When you're sympathetic you step outside it.

Being present

Being present is central to masterful coaching. You need to focus all your attention on your client. This sounds easy in principle and is more difficult in practice. Without you even realizing it your mind drifts away – you suddenly catch yourself mentally writing a shopping list or thinking about the romantic dinner you had last night

When that happens just bring your attention back. People sense if you're not fully engaged and start to wonder what's going on

– especially if it's a regular occurrence or you're 'away' too long.

Sometimes it's because the room's warm and airless or you're tired and weary. But occasionally it's because you're bored – especially if they're repeating something you've heard before. What the client's saying really doesn't interest you. Yes, it's a shocking thought, and you may not want to admit it to yourself. But it happens. And if it's true your client will realize at some level and rapport will vanish – and so might they!

When you notice the discussion not holding your attention you need to bring about a change or the relationship will suffer. Ask another question. Get them to take a different perspective. If you're not present, you're not actually there for the person.

Decreasing rapport

There are times, you may be surprised to hear, when you want to decrease the rapport you have with your client. The most common is when you're coming to the end of a session and they're still in full flow – and oblivious to the time. Now you could just interrupt them. But even if you do it nicely it can seem rude. So you might like to consider some non-verbal options, such as sitting up in more of a 'ready-to-go' pose or starting to gather together any papers you might have. Some clients register these signals at an unconscious level and realize it's time to go.

In phone coaching there are no visual cues for them to pick up on. So you need to do it by means of voice tone. Switching to a slightly more business-like, matter-of-fact intonation often does the trick, as does simply acknowledging them –'Excellent', 'Okay' – rather than asking further questions.

Another, different, situation in which it's useful to reduce the rapport you have is when clients start to think of you as a friend rather than as a coach. It's easy for this to happen, particularly in life coaching where the person often discusses intimate aspects of their experience they've never shared with anyone else. Clients can easily mistake your warmth and empathy as something more than a professional interest. If you feel they're getting too familiar and intimate you need to create and enforce a strict boundary.

In our experience it's difficult to be an effective coach with a friend, and there needs to be a degree of distance for the relationship to deliver results.

Taking notes during a session

Should you make notes when coaching? Many coaches prefer not to when working face-to-face because every time they look down at the paper and write they disconnect from their client. Their attention is divided and they're no longer observing and listening to them.

This can be distracting and disruptive for clients and they may even lose their train of thought while they politely wait for you to finish scribbling. Some coaches find it useful to make brief notes during the session of the main points, to act as a skeleton onto which flesh can be added after the session.

If you prefer not to make notes during the session you can always jot down the main headlines afterwards. But there's always a danger of you missing something out, especially if it's been a long session, and significant details will almost certain be omitted.

Whether or not you decide to jot things down is less of an issue in phone coaching. Clients can't see what you're doing. So it's much easier to make notes as you go along. However they will notice if you sound distracted, so keep them brief.

When rapport is missing

But what do you do when, despite your best efforts, rapport is missing? You just don't seem to 'hit it off'. Well, that's a tough call. If there's no rapport there's no real coaching relationship. And you're unlikely to be able to achieve very much if anything together.

But there are limits to your ability to enhance rapport. And if you reach the point where you've tried everything and there's still little if any connection between you it's probably best if you decide to go your separate ways. Your first responsibility is to the client, and they may be able to find someone who they can work better with than you.

Sometimes that's not an option. If you're working as a business coach or in-company, your client may have no choice about working with you – and had you 'thrust' upon them. If they feel you've been brought in to 'fix' them they'll often be defensive – and rapport will be elusive to say the least. We'll be discussing what to do when the client's not engaged in the coaching in Chapter 16.

Occasionally – but rarely – you may be uncomfortable in the presence of your client. You may feel physically uneasy or emotionally on edge. This is not the basis for an effective coaching relationship, and you should seek to end the relationship as soon as possible.

Losing rapport

What do you do if you had good rapport with a client and it starts to disappear? Almost certainly something is wrong and you need to take action. The first step is to find out what's going on. It may have been something you've inadvertently said or done they're not happy about.

Or perhaps they're not making the progress they hoped. Discovering the root cause may be all that's necessary. The relationship could then heal itself. If it's a more fundamental problem you will have to decide what to do on a case-by-case basis. The best approach is usually to get the issue out in the open and discuss it with your client.

Summary

Whether you coach face to face or by telephone, enhancing your rapport skills will help you to become more effective. When you meet your client in their 'model of the world' – by starting from where they're at – and match what you do and say with the how they take in and process information, you will connect with them more fully and deeply.

What you can do

- Every time you make a phone call over the next week, make a note of the things you can detect about the person's voice.
- Practise your rapport skills on a daily basis.
- Constantly refine what you do so that your ability to achieve a connection with people is continually improving.
- Try out different forms of note-taking and decide which is right for you.

10
coaching frameworks and models

In this chapter you will learn:
- how to use structures to get you started in coaching
- about the GROW model
- how to use the S.C.O.R.E. model
- about other models used by coaches
- about coaching in the moment.

Having a framework to follow

When you first start coaching it can all feel a bit daunting – perhaps even scary. Your client is sitting opposite you and looking at you expectantly. Or you answer the phone to begin a telephone session. How do you get things off on a good footing? What question do you ask next? How do you keep things moving along? And what do you do when you don't know what to do?

Most new coaches lack confidence in the early days. And it's only natural. There's so much to think about, and always the fear of messing up and appearing unprofessional. So it can be reassuring to have a structure you can follow as you're gaining experience – like having stabilizers on a bicycle for support when you're learning to ride.

In this chapter we're going to introduce you to a number of models and frameworks you can use while you're cutting your coaching teeth – including the well known GROW and Inner Game models. Some people continue to use such frameworks even when they've got a lot of coaching under their belt, while others 'take the stabilizers off' as their confidence grows. The Co-active model, which we'll also be discussing, offers no steps or sequences at all – just a free-flowing approach to coaching based around a set of tools and techniques. If you seem to know instinctively what to say and do from the word go, or have a preference for doing things your own way rather than following a procedure, this is for you. Others will want to work up to it.

GROW

The GROW model provides a simple sequence of steps you can follow. It was developed by Sir John Whitmore in the 1980s and is detailed in his ground-breaking book *Coaching for Performance* (1999). GROW is widely used in business, and its structured approach can be extremely effective. The acronym stands for Goal, Reality, Options and What Will You Do. You'll also see the model with a 'T' added to the front (TGROW), which stands for the Topic the client wants to work on. Our description here is of the original model.

Goal

To avoid it becoming just a cosy chat, you need to establish with your client a clear, specific goal for the session. This helps ensure you don't go off track. A client may have all kinds of things in mind, such as becoming clear about an issue, exploring the dynamics of a troublesome relationship or finding ways to reduce the amount of time spent in unproductive meetings.

Sample dialogue

Coach: What do you want to get out of this session?

Client: I can't get on with my boss. He's a nightmare to work for, and seems to single me out whenever anything goes wrong. I want to find a better way of dealing with him.

Coach: What precisely do you mean by better?

Client: I guess I need a strategy for handling his behaviour that leaves me feeling in control of the situation.

There will be much more detail on goal-setting in Chapter 11.

Reality

Having established the goal you then ask your client questions so you understand as objectively as possible the current Reality. 'Coaches should use', says Whitmore, 'and as far as possible encourage the coachee to use, descriptive rather than evaluative terminology'. The aim is to avoid distortion by staying detached – free of any judgement about what's right or wrong, good or bad. You might think of yourself as a detective, seeking out reliable evidence in the form of facts, figures and information that can be verified. You should also listen out for clues that point to promising lines of investigation and inconsistencies that don't ring true. The questions you ask should encourage your client to think as deeply as possible – getting to the heart of the issue and bringing to awareness new insights. Your aim is to address the cause not just the symptom. Concentrate on Who, What, Where and When questions, avoiding Why and How – which lead to a defensive, justifying response in the former and analysis in the latter.

Sample dialogue

Coach: So, we've established your goal. Let's explore what's happening now. You say your boss singles you out when things go wrong. When does this happen?

Client: All the time.

Coach: Every minute, every hour of every day?

Client: Well, no, it is not that bad. I guess it's mostly at the end of the month, when all the project progress reports need to be in.

Coach: What happens at that time?

Client: I'm working like mad to gather the data together quickly. It's a bit like being in a pressure cooker. (voice changes) That's when I usually get the call to go to the boss's office.

Coach: It doesn't sound like you're getting much help. Who else is around in the office at the time?

Client: Just my small team – that's Ann who looks after administration and Dave does finance. They're generally busy with the day-to-day work. Besides, by the time I've explained it to them, I might as well have done it myself.

Coach: What stops you preparing some of this in advance?

Client: There's just not enough time – especially if we've got a big project on.

Coach: Okay. Tell me what happens when you get the call from your boss.

Client: I go in and he reads me the riot act. Then I start to get upset and can't get my words out clearly. It all comes out wrong.

Coach: What are you thinking about?

Client: I'm worrying about whether or not I'll get fired this time.

Coach: What does your boss actually want you to do?

Client: (Pauses) I suppose he wants the report to arrive on time so he doesn't get it in the neck from the managing director.

The dialogue would continue, with the coach and client gathering further detail about what's happening.

Options

How many different solutions can your client come up with? The aim isn't to come up with a course of action that's 'right' or 'perfect' – at least not straight away. Don't allow your client to limit themselves. The more choices they generate the better. Quantity is much more important than quality during the options phase.

Get them to start by brain-dumping everything that seems obvious – then push them to be even more creative. It's all too easy for clients to dismiss ideas or not have them in the first place because they believe they can't be done or won't work. Get them to dig deep to generate every choice available – and then some. Make it clear that suggestions which seem silly, crazy or simply off-the-wall are not only acceptable – they're compulsory! There should be no censorship or inhibition whatsoever when coming up with options.

Like all of us, clients hold all sorts of irrational, limiting beliefs, of which they are often unaware. You'll hear: 'There isn't the budget' or 'I could never learn to do that'. When you hear the word 'can't' get them to turn it into a 'can' by challenging them to think of a way round the block or over the obstacle that's getting in the way. One way to do this is to ask 'What if' questions – 'What if you could learn?' or 'What if you did have the budget?'

You can also help by encouraging your client to break large issues into smaller chunks. This will make the process feel more manageable. It's a bit like trying to swallow an elephant whole – it's easier one bite at a time.

Sample dialogue

Coach: What different strategies can you think of that will leave you feeling in control of the situation?

Client: Well, while we've been talking I've been wondering how I can get Ann and Dave more involved instead of feeling I have to do it all myself. Perhaps Dave could look after the budget figures and I could ask Ann to manage the performance studies. Then I can take care of the rest.

Coach: Great. What else can you do?

Client: I could develop a simple computer-based system for people to record the information online, which will save us all time chasing people for it. I've thought about that before but not put any energy into it.

Coach: What else?

Client: I need to manage my boss's expectations better, and agree an extension when there's a big project to do.

Coach: Well you've certainly got some good ideas. Is that it?

Client: (Pauses) I need to learn to trust Ann and Dave to play their part in the whole thing.

Coach: That sounds good. Is there another option you could come up with that is more of a stretch?

Client: If I explain the whole process to Ann and Dave they may be able to cover for me when I'm immersed in a big project.

Coach: Yes, that would be a stretch and it could save you a lot of time in the long run.

The discussion continues until several more, increasingly creative, options are generated.

What WILL you do?

This is the 'Will' step in which the client makes a decision and constructs an action plan. It's also sometimes referred to as the 'What next?', 'Way Forward' or even the 'Wrap-up'. It's when the best ideas from the options phase are selected and turned into reality.

There are various questions you can ask to support your client in considering the options and making the choice that's best for them. Whitmore suggests the following nine as a 'backbone', to be supplemented by secondary questions of your own.

1 What are you actually going to do?
2 When are you going to do it?
3 Will this action meet your goal?
4 What obstacles might you meet along the way?
5 Who needs to know?
6 What support do you need?
7 How and when are you going to get that support?
8 What other considerations do you have?
9 On a 1 to 10 scale, what degree of certainty do you have that you will carry out the actions agreed?

(Whitmore, 1999)

Clients are often all fired up once they start to formulate their plans. Some will immediately ask themselves what might hold them back and others overlook any potential obstacles there might be along the way. It's the coach's job to check they think everything through. Some people, for instance, assume they have to do everything themselves when there may be plenty of support available to help them. The question about 'other considerations' is important as a safety net to make sure nothing of consequence gets missed. Working through these questions carefully will ensure that options are thoroughly evaluated and plans put into place to bring those chosen to fruition. Often more than one of the ideas generated will be incorporated into the solution ultimately arrived at.

Sample dialogue
Coach: Right this is the list of things you came up with:
• Getting Dave and Ann involved in the short term – Ann on

performance and Dave doing the budgets.
- Computer-based record system.
- Managing the boss's expectations.
- Agreeing an extension in advance when there are big projects to do.
- Trusting Ann and Dave.
- Training Ann and Dave to cover for you when needed.

Which of these are you actually going to do?

Client: I'm definitely going to get Ann and Dave involved, starting with next month's report.

Coach: When are you going to tell them about it?

Client: The sooner the better – first thing tomorrow morning.

Coach: What about the other things on your list?

Client: The computer system feels like a long-term project to me. I know I keep putting if off because it's going to take time to think it through.

Coach: You mentioned trusting Ann and Dave. How could you do that more?

Client: Well, Ann's good at organizing things and pretty good with computers, so I could delegate the thinking through to her. (Pauses) Yes, she certainly enjoys a challenge. I'll talk to her about it. It will demonstrate that I'm prepared to trust her with something important too.

Coach: When are you going to do that?

Client: At our weekly meeting next Friday.

Coach: What about your longer term idea of training Ann and Dave to cover for you?

Client: I think I'd like to see how they get on with this for now and come back to that later.

Coach: I'll hold you to that.

Client: I thought you might.

Coach: How much later?

Client: Not too long. I'll review it at the end of next month.

Coach: What about your boss?

Client: I have a feeling that most of the problems will disappear once I've put these things in place. I'll definitely let him know in advance if I foresee any problems.

Coach: How far in advance?

Client: At least two weeks before.

Coach: If you put all of this into place, will it meet your goal?

Client: It's better than I dared imagine. I can't wait to get started.

Coach: What obstacles do you think you will come across?

Client: There could be some technical hitches with the computer system which I need to run past the IT department. The rest seems pretty straightforward.

Coach: Who needs to know about all this?

Client: Ann and Dave, of course. The guys in IT. Our contacts in other departments who supply us with the information.

Coach: What about your boss?

Client: Yes, him too.

Coach: What support will you need?

Client: I'm pretty sure the boss will support the plan because it takes the problem away for him. He could help influence the other departments if I get any kick-back about the new approach.

Coach: On a 1 to 10 scale, what degree of certainty do you have that you will carry all this out?

Client: Around 7–8 overall, because I'm bound to hit some snags along the way which could slow things down. In the long term though it's a 10.

At the end of the session it may be useful to make a note of what the client has decided to do – by when, overcoming what obstacles and with whose support. This will help you to monitor progress in future sessions.

Coaching sessions vary enormously and you'll sometimes find the client resists making changes or doesn't decide to follow through with every idea on the list of options.

From linear to flexible

Using any new process can feel strange at first but with practice you'll soon become fluent with GROW to the point where you hardly think about it at all. Initially, you'll probably follow a linear sequence, going from G→R→O→W, but the model is meant to be used flexibly. This means, for instance, you can start with Reality – where the client is now – instead of Goal – where they want to be.

However they may be tempted to go for small, incremental steps, rather than bigger leaps, and set goals based on what has gone before, rather than on what might be possible or desirable.

You need to guard against them setting the bar too low (there's more about this in Chapter 15).

If you rush any of the stages you may find you have to backtrack and revisit some of them. While it's okay to do that your aim is to take as much time as your client needs. When you've used the model for a while you'll start to pick up clues through what your client says – and by paying attention to their body language – that tells you they're ready to move on.

Outgrowing GROW

GROW can be a good starting point, but it isn't the be-all and end-all of coaching. Its emphasis on choosing and achieving goals makes it suitable for some, but not all, issues, while its prescriptive nature makes it restricting for those who like to think for themselves. When followed slavishly it may become a strait-jacket rather than a structure. If you find this to be the case, do not be afraid to try other models.

The S.C.O.R.E. model

S.C.O.R.E. is not strictly a coaching model, but it can be adapted and used successfully – giving more flexibility than GROW. S.C.O.R.E. was conceived in 1987 by NLP developers Robert Dilts and Todd Epstein as a more effective and sophisticated way of bringing about personal change.

The traditional model of change featured three elements: the Present State (How things are now); the Desired State (How we want things to be); and the Solution (What needs to happen to bring the Desired State about). These distinctions, Dilts and Epstein discovered, offered insufficient differentiation, and they split 'Present State' into 'Symptoms' and 'Causes', and 'Desired State' into 'Outcomes' and 'Effects'. 'Solution' is renamed 'Resources', and the letters combined to give the acronym S.C.O.R.E. These elements, according to the model, represent the minimum amount of information that needs to be addressed by any process of change. The advantage of S.C.O.R.E. is that it's loose and fluid. You can start anywhere and go anywhere – zig-zagging back and forth as often as you like.

Symptoms

Often you'll start with the Symptom – the problem, issue etc. It's *what's wrong* with your client: 'I'm not hitting my sales targets'; 'I'm eating too much chocolate'. You can find out more about the Symptom by asking the following kinds of questions:

- What's the problem?
- What do you want to change?
- What's wrong?

Outcomes

Sometimes, though, it's the Outcome that comes first – the goal or result the client wants to achieve. 'I want to buy a bigger house'; 'I want to be happy'. It's having unfulfilled dreams and desires that often drives people to seek out coaching. To learn more about their Outcomes ask these kinds of questions:

- What do you want?
- What are your dreams?
- What is your goal?

Effects

However, it's useful for a coach to be aware that Outcomes are not always an end in themself. They may be stepping stones on the road to other Outcomes. So there's great value in asking a client why they want to achieve a particular goal – what its Effect will be. You can use this information to apply leverage and motivate your client to achieve what they want. The example below illustrates how this works:

- The effect of your client's outcome of going to the gym might be to 'appear more attractive'.
- The effect of 'appearing more attractive' might be to 'find a life partner'.
- And the effect of 'finding a life partner' might be 'to be happy'.

Sometimes the Effect of an Outcome will be negative, and can sometimes provide an insight into why the client has not yet achieved it. They might say they want promotion – and keep 'getting turned down'. This may be because they're unconsciously sabotaging the process. Part of them wants the new job and part of them 'knows' the Effect would be to work longer hours and see less of the family.

Questions relating to Effects include:

• What will you get from achieving your goal?
• How will this outcome benefit you?
• Why is this important to you?

Causes

Because coaching tends to have an Outcome Focus rather than a Problem Focus, time and effort is rarely spent understanding the Cause of a particular issue. But treating a Symptom will only bring temporary relief. Drinking lots of coffee will give someone with low energy a boost, but won't tackle the cause, which may be insufficient sleep, over-work or both. Slashing prices, for instance, may in the short-term help counter falling sales, but it doesn't get to the root of the issue, which may be that the product or service needs revamping or better marketing.

• What's at the root of the problem?
• What do you think is causing this?

Resources

The aim, ultimately, of the S.C.O.R.E. model is to help the client find the necessary Resources that will produce an effective solution – whether that be to remove a Symptom or achieve an Outcome. Resources could be many things: tools and techniques, support from others, changing a limiting belief, introducing some form of structure or developing new habits. Taking a training course may be the best and simplest 'Resource', for instance, if your client wants to improve their presentation skills.

The Inner Game

Tim Gallwey, author of *The Inner Game* series of books, developed a method of improving personal performance in sports and then went on to transfer his approach to the world of work.

'Coaching,' says Gallwey (2000), 'is unlocking a person's potential to maximize their own performance. It is helping them to learn rather than teaching them.'

He argued that we all have two games we play: an Outer Game against our opponent and an Inner Game played out in our heads against a part of us that tries hard, over-analyses and thinks too much. You can't win the Outer Game until you've won the Inner Game. And the way to do that is to remove the interference we're creating that stops us achieving our potential.

$$P = p - i$$

Performance = potential − interference

'Trying Fails, Awareness Cures,' asserts Gallwey (2000). The interference disappears when, instead of trying, you increase your awareness and focus your attention on something relevant in the environment.

Some coaches work exclusively from an Inner Game model. They help their clients to cultivate non-judgemental awareness, which drives out the interference. Gallwey discovered that when he asked tennis players to pay attention to the ball, noticing which way it was spinning and how high it was bouncing, rather than on the 'right way' to swing the racket, they hit it more accurately.

Inner Game coaching can be applied to a wide range of situations, including improving relationships, losing weight, leading a team, writing novels, sales skills and public speaking. Tim Gallwey describes his coaching model in the following way: 'Effective coaching in the workplace holds a mirror up for clients, so they can see their own thinking process. As a coach I'm not listening for the content of what's being said as much as I'm listening to the way they are thinking, including how their attention is focused and how they define the key elements of the situation.'

Skilled Helper

Gerard Egan, like Dilts and Epstein, has also further developed the traditional three-stage change model. He gives the stages of the model slightly different names: Stage I – The current state of affairs, Stage II – The preferred scenario and Stage III – Strategies for Action. Although this model is more widely used in counselling, it also has value when it comes to coaching. It contains steps within each stage that once again are meant to be used in a fluid fashion. Each stage is further broken down into three steps as follows:

Stage I The current state of affairs

1 The coach encourages the client to get a clear picture of their issue by asking them to tell a story about what's going on.
2 The coach goes on to help their client uncover blind spots and open up new perspectives.
3 Then the coach helps the client choose the right issues to work on – the ones that make the biggest difference, or leverage personal change.

Stage II The preferred scenario

1 The coach encourages the client to come up with possible solutions to their problem.
2 The client goes on to select and prioritize realistic and stretching goals – this is known as exploring the change agenda.
3 The coach tests the client's commitment to follow their ideas through into action.

Stage III Strategies for action

1 The coach makes sure the client has discovered how to get what they need and want by examining possible actions they can take.
2 Then the client chooses the best-fit for them – in terms of time, resources available and so on.
3 The actions are organized into a plan they can follow.

Any stage can lead to actions that help the individual achieve the outcome they want and the coach (or helper as Egan describes them) is meant to use this in a flexible way to match the needs of their clients. As Egan (1998) says, 'clients do not always present all their problems in neat packages'. This means you'll find it virtually impossible to complete Stage I without dipping into the other two stages first. Another feature of this model is that it encourages ongoing evaluation throughout rather than leaving all the testing to the end.

> *'Dogmatic adherence to a single model or a consultant-centered process will doom authentic coaching.'*
> David M. Noer (1999)

Co-active coaching

While S.C.O.R.E., GROW, Inner Game and Skilled Helper are all useful models – especially when you first start to coach – ultimately they limit your versatility and flexibility. And they can be a distraction. You need to be focused on your client and not the model you're using. If your mind is on the process it's not on the person – and that's not what coaching is about.

The model that we subscribe to, and which forms the basis of this book and of much contemporary coaching practice in general is the Co-active Coaching model developed by The Coaches Training Institute in the 1990s. This was followed by a book by Laura Whitworth called *Co-active Coaching: New Skills for Coaching People Toward Success in Work and Life* (1998). The book describes the model as having four cornerstones:

1 The client is creative, resourceful and whole.
2 Co-active coaching addresses the client's whole life.
3 The agenda comes from the client.
4 The relationship is a designed alliance.

The name Co-active arises from the fact that it involves an active and collaborative partnership between the coach and the client. The authors describe it as 'an alliance of equals'. Coaching covers the client's whole life – they look at the big picture not just the detail in part of their client's life. The coach is totally focused on the client – this means listening without judgement to not just the words but the meaning behind them.

Co-active coaches work on the basis that people have the ability to resolve their issues and achieve their dreams. They know what's important to their clients and 'hold it true' for them. They're prepared to challenge and tell their clients the truth.

Coaching as improvisation

What's great about the Co-active model is that it doesn't have any prescribed steps or processes.

Budding musicians generally start by learning songs note by note, playing them the same every single time. But as they progress they get to the stage where they have the experience to improvise – making decisions in the moment about what to do and where to go next.

Coaching can be like that too. When you first attempt to coach without the aid of a model it can feel uncomfortable – as if your safety net has been taken away. What if you 'fall'– and there's an embarrassing silence with you floundering around 'um-ing' and 'ah-ing'.

If you're telephone coaching there's an easy way round this. Keep a list of stock coaching questions beside you so you can draw upon them if you get stuck. When you're coaching face-to-face you can hardly have scraps of paper around with 'prompts' on them – it doesn't exactly inspire confidence – but you can store a few 'get you out of trouble' questions at the back of your mind in case you ever need them (see Chapter 12 for lots more on questioning).

But you probably won't. Coaches quickly learn to 'fly solo' and soon look back and wonder what they were worried about. The more coaching you have under your belt the more confident you'll get. And you'll only ever achieve mastery if you give up following a 'script' and try something like the Co-active approach. Once you start it you'll never look back because it brings freedom and flexibility for the coach and amazing results for the client.

What you can do

- Practise using the GROW model in a flexible way until you can move in and out of each stage effortlessly.
- Try out the S.C.O.R.E. model with someone you know well as many times as you need to until you get the hang of it.
- Take a risk and have a go at coaching without any pre-formed structure – all you have to do is focus on your client and trust that the right question will be in your mind when you need it.

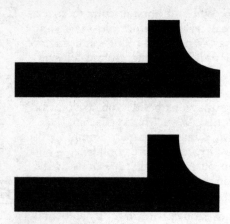

11

good coaching practice

In this chapter you will learn:

- how to work with your client to set clear goals
- how to get off to a good start each session
- how to manage the flow of coaching
- how to deal with 'bumps' and 'gremlins'
- the mindset of an effective coach
- the value of redesigning the alliance
- logistical issues to consider.

The second session

So – you've run your intake session, and you've got a good understanding of frameworks you can use and you're about to start your second session. What are you going to do? How do you plan to use the time? And what will you do in the sessions that follow? This is where new coaches sometimes struggle. It's one thing knowing how the pieces move in chess but quite another actually playing a game. Once you've done a few sessions it gets easier – you know the ropes and have more confidence in what you're doing.

Setting goals

One obvious place to start is with the Primary Focus list drawn up in the first session. Which item would your client like to work on first? Most people will know immediately, but some will deliberate for a moment before deciding. The next step is to transform what's often a vague goal into something more precise. Often the reason your client hasn't achieved it already is because they don't know in detail what they want. Perhaps it's to 'lose weight' or 'earn more' but these statements are not specific enough to be of any real use.

SMART

For a goal to be motivating and effective it needs to be sharply defined. One model that's widely used in business, and which some clients will have heard of and maybe even used, is SMART, which stands for:

Specific – what precisely do you want? And when, where and how? Define the goal as specifically and narrowly as possible.

Measurable – a goal is meaningless if you can't determine whether you've achieved it or not. So make it quantifiable, so you can measure success.

Achievable or Agreed – it's important to set the goal at the right level: if it's too easy the results won't be much to write home about, but if it's too hard your client may not even try because they know they'll fall short. Goals need to be challenging but achievable – and under the client's control. (Performance-related goals in the workplace are also usually agreed with a manager).

Relevant – is the goal appropriate for the purpose in mind? Does it directly address the problem? If not the goal needs to be refined or changed.

Time bound – by when will the goal be achieved? It's essential to get this right. If the date is too far off it won't be motivating. If my plan were to lose 14 pounds in five years' time, I'm unlikely to take much action towards it now. If it's too close, it's not even worth trying. Lose 14 pounds in 14 days? I don't think so!

Work through the five elements of SMART with your client, making sure they are clear about each one.

In the example below a manager has set the following SMART goal:

'I want to deliver a ten-minute presentation confidently, without notes, by the 4 June.'

- The goal is specific because she's given precise details of what she wants.
- The goal is measurable in two ways: it has to be done without notes and with a feeling of confidence (which will also be evident to an audience).
- The goal is achievable – others have done it – but for this manager it's challenging.
- Since the manager has a need to speak in public, the goal can be considered relevant.
- The 4 June is the date when she will have achieved her goal.

Well-formed outcomes

An even more detailed process for clarifying goals comes from Neuro-Linguistic Programming. In NLP goals are known as 'outcomes', and it's considered essential that they be 'Well Formed' – that is, they meet a set of rigorous criteria designed to increase the likelihood of their success. The Well-Formed Outcome conditions are as follows:

1 State the outcome in positive terms – say what you want rather than what you don't want.
2 Ensure the outcome is within your control – are you able to do it without anyone else being involved?
3 Be as specific as possible – the more precise you are the better.
4 Have a sensory-based evidence procedure – creating a mental image of having the outcome can be a useful way of gathering the information you need.
5 Consider the context – when, where and with whom do you want the outcome?

6 Have access to resources – these can be internal, such as a memory of feeling confident, or external, such as receiving help from someone else.

7 Ensure the outcome preserves existing benefits – the reason we don't always make a change in our behaviour is because of a benefit that the old behaviour gives us.

8 Check the outcome is ecologically sound – explore the bigger picture and ask yourself, 'If I had it would I really want it?'

9 Define the first step – if you don't take action, it will remain nothing more than a dream.

It may seem a laborious process working through all nine steps – and it certainly takes a reasonable chunk of time. But it's time well spent. By digging deep into each of the conditions in turn you create in effect a strategy for achieving the outcome. And you often uncover the reasons why your client hasn't achieved it yet – sometimes despite years of trying.

Towards and away from

Not everyone, however, is motivated by moving towards goals and outcomes. Some people are energized by moving away from problems and difficulties. And talking in terms of 'achieving' won't rejuvenate them much at all. They're more concerned with avoiding pain than gaining pleasure.

Personal development guru Tony Robbins expresses the power of this principle well in his book *Awaken the Giant Within* (1992): 'Understanding and utilizing the forces of pain and pleasure will allow you once and for all to create the lasting changes and improvements you desire for yourself and those you care about.'

So make sure you understand what motivates your clients – and what makes a course of action compelling for them. Some people leave their job because they can't stand it any more (moving away from pain). Others because they've found a position they like more (moving towards pleasure).

Pain sometimes also stops us doing things. We keep putting off writing that report because we know it's going to be a hard slog. But the day before it's due we suddenly knuckle down and do it – because the pain of doing it is not as great as the pain of not doing it. The boss will want to know where it is and is likely to be annoyed if it's not done on time.

When goals seem too big

Goals can sometimes be too big to be motivating – simply because they're so overwhelming. A client wanting to get fit might decide it would be a good idea to run a marathon to give themselves something to aim for. But the idea of covering 26 miles can seem unattainable so they never set foot out of the door. Many people like the idea of writing a book, but when they think of having to come up with a 70,000 word manuscript it all seems too much. But if you work with your client to break down big goals into sub-goals they often make dynamic changes. Instead of focusing on a marathon, they might focus on a 3 mile 'fun run' to start with. Or aim to write just a 2,000 word sample chapter of the book.

Steve was working with a client who consistently, over a period of time, failed to move forward with a range of different projects, including writing and personal goals As she was encouraged to 'dig into' the problem during the coaching, it became apparent that the goals she'd set herself seemed so enormous she didn't know where to start – so she ended up taking no action at all. By working back from her goal, and breaking it down into smaller chunks, she came up with sub-goals she felt she could tackle comfortably. The following session, having finally made a start, she was full of energy and excitement, and she moved forward effectively from there.

How would you like to spend the time?

It's also worth saying there's more to coaching than goals. While many of the people you work with will want to achieve certain things, such as doubling their turnover or halving their debt, others will simply want to explore issues, such as what they should do with their life or whether they're in the right relationship. And even when clients are looking to achieve certain goals, not every moment of every session will be focused relentlessly on working towards them.

Sometimes you'll be considering options and evaluating choices. The most important thing is that you always work to an agenda that's set by the client not by you. The coach's role is to create a 'space' in which they can discuss whatever's of interest or concern to them without direction from you.

Some clients arrive for their second session and wait expectantly for you to kick the meeting off. And that's when you can ask a really simple question: 'How would you like to spend the time today?'

This does two things. First it focuses their attention on what precisely they want to get out of the session – preventing it rambling on without direction. And, second, it communicates to the client loud and clear that the responsibility for what goes on rests fairly and squarely with them.

Clients move on

What's even more important is to continue to ask that question at the beginning of subsequent sessions. That's because it's all too easy to assume they want to continue where they left off – when they may be done with that issue or it no longer seems pressing. People often move on between sessions. You can't just start from where they were last time. You have to check where they're at every single occasion.

But if you're not careful you can get caught out. Clients can launch straight in with a barrage of information, hardly stopping to draw breath. You can spend a lot of time listening to your clients giving you chapter and verse about what's happened since you last met. Sometimes all it takes is a seemingly innocent question, 'How did you get on since last week?' Before you know it 15 minutes have disappeared. Or they start by reporting on the 'homework' you gave them and once again a chunk of the session has been used up.

As a coach you need to manage the time and encourage your clients to do the same. What they're sharing may be valuable, but you have a limited period together and every minute needs to be used wisely. So don't hesitate to interrupt them – nicely of course – to ask the 'How would you like...?' question. If you don't the conversation could easily go off at a tangent. If they insist on updating you it's a good idea to agree a time limit with them so they get best value from the time you have together.

Some clients deal with the same issue all the way through. Others flit back and forth between the various items on their Primary Focus list. It's like a dance in which the client leads and the coach follows – but always gracefully and elegantly, and hopefully without stepping on their toes.

The coach does this principally by asking questions which facilitate that process. We'll be looking at the art of asking questions, and listening carefully to the answers, in Chapter 12, and some of the techniques can be found in Chapter 13.

Be prepared for the unexpected

As your session progresses you may find your client suddenly comes up with a topic that's completely new. They've never mentioned it before. It appears to have come in from 'left field'. That's one of the challenges – and pleasures – of coaching you never know what's going to happen next. So you should always be prepared for the unexpected.

If the new subject matter seems to be way off track in relation to the goals they originally expressed you'll want to point that out. That may not matter to them. It may have just become significant in their life – a call from a head-hunter opens a new door, or a fight with a loved one potentially closes another one. Ultimately, the decision about what gets discussed lies with the client – not with the coach.

The flow of coaching

In the first couple of sessions there's normally lots of energy, excitement and euphoria, especially if the person's never had coaching before. You can almost see light bulbs getting switched on in their head and sparks flying in every direction. That often continues into subsequent sessions, but sometimes, after the fourth time you get together, things seem to slow down.

Occasionally it can feel as though you've hit a plateau, as the initial 'adrenaline rush' of change and discovery gets replaced by a sense of routine and the rate of progress is markedly reduced.

This doesn't always happen. Some coaching relationships maintain the early enthusiasm and go from strength to strength. But most eventually hit a sticky patch. This can be worrying for rookie coaches who can start to doubt their own abilities. But there's usually no fundamental problem. It's pretty much par for the course. All you need is a steady nerve and a stabilizing hand on the tiller to navigate the choppy waters.

One step forward, two steps back

Indeed, as we suggested in Chapter 8, it's a good idea to tell your client during the Intake Session there will inevitably be some 'bumps along the way'. That way they won't be concerned when they materialize – and neither will you.

When we think about achieving a goal we tend to imagine it being a linear process which involves getting there in the minimum amount of time by taking the fastest possible route – like whizzing down the motorway between two cities. But life – and coaching – isn't always like that. For a variety of reasons we often we end up taking the 'scenic' route – zig-zagging our way across the countryside at a leisurely pace before arriving at our destination.

You need to make sure your clients understand that progress is unlikely to be smooth and direct. There may be times when nothing seems to happen, times when they take one step forward and two steps back, and times when things seem to loop around in circles. This is perfectly natural and normal. Rather than being afraid of it, or embarrassed, discuss it with your client, asking 'What's going on here?'.

Dealing with 'gremlins'

Sometimes what happens is that it's one of your client's many 'gremlins' that's getting in the way. A 'gremlin' is a voice inside your head that gives you a hard time. 'You could have done that better', 'You'll never be any good at that', 'You can't paint/draw/sing/play football...'

Gremlins don't like change. They want to maintain the status quo. And they often fight hard and dirty to safeguard it, sabotaging progress your clients desperately want to make. They're likely to recognize this 'internal critic' and may even, with a little help from you, come to realize that their gremlins have a positive intention – perhaps to keep them safe or prevent them from feeling foolish. A 'gremlin' is not the person themself because people are able to mentally stand back and observe their 'gremlins' behaviour.

The more your clients become aware of their gremlins the closer they are to dealing with them. But it's not easy. Gremlins are tricky and slippery. For more on this subject take a look at *Taming Your Gremlin* (1990) by Richard Carson. It's a fascinating read and will give you strategies for bringing your clients' gremlins out of the shadows where they can be examined in the cold light of day.

Tolerance of frustration

Clients vary in their ability to tolerate frustration. Some have a high threshold, cope well with getting stuck and making slow progress, and take it in their stride. People with Low Frustration Tolerance (LFT) have difficulty handling frustration and setbacks, and may become difficult to coach when things get tough. If that's the case you need to find a way of getting out of the 'rut' – and fast – if the relationship is not to break down and come to an end.

You might come up with some possible ideas to stimulate discussion, rather than leaving it all to the other person. Or even use some specific techniques – such as Perceptual Positions or Using Metaphors – designed to 'jump start' the coaching (see Chapter 13). If you're familiar with any profiling tools and you haven't used them, now would be a good time to introduce them.

But whatever you do, make sure you remain focused on your client's agenda. Don't get pulled off track and feel you have to start providing direction for the sessions. That's not your role.

In between homework and assignments

One useful way of keeping things moving is to ask your client if they would be interested in doing some 'homework' between sessions. If they're agreeable, there's a wide range of things you could get them to do – such as list 50 things they want, or observe how other people behave when meeting for the first time. Anything that's relevant to their issues and goals is worth trying. Not everyone is willing to take on out-of-session activities – but many are keen to maximize the value they get from the coaching and are happy to agree.

The mindset and manner of the coach

Throughout your sessions, from Intake through to Completion, you should evidence as many of the qualities listed in Chapter 2 of the ideal coach. Foremost among these is arguably curiosity. Having a deep, genuine desire to understand your client, without preconception or prejudice, will sustain most coaching relationships through the ups and downs that are usually experienced.

Humour, too, as long as it doesn't trivialize or is insensitive, can be a great tool. Although coaching is, at heart, a serious business, having a light touch can work wonders when it comes to trying new things or taking risks. Being earnest and ponderous creates a different energy, and one that's rarely conducive to masterful coaching.

And we can't say often enough how important it is for you to be compassionate, tolerant and understanding of the people you work with. As well as being respectful of them as individuals it's certain to pay dividends in terms of their willingness to engage with the process.

Giving positive support

One other thing that really works is staying positive. This can give your clients wings when all else seems to fail. The act of acknowledging some quality or characteristic they have, for instance, effectively moves them forward as they become stronger and more resourceful. And championing them even when they stop believing in their own ability for a while lets them know you're 'fighting their corner'. You might say, 'It may not feel like it right now but you will come through this' or, 'You're so close to completing it I know you can get there.' When the going gets tough you may be the only person who will remind them they can still attain their goal.

Redesigning the alliance

The nature of the coaching alliance is that it's meant to be re-designed on an on-going basis. Working in this way encourages the client to take responsibility for their own experience during coaching sessions. The client could ask the coach to behave in a different way or give them some feedback and leave them to decide how to adjust their approach. Some clients may want more time to think, for instance, and ask their coach to leave longer gaps before asking the next question. Others might ask the coach to contribute ideas from time to time.

The coach will generally need to remind the client to do this – at least to start off with. Reviews are a regular part of the coaching relationship. Once you've designed the way you're going to work with each other it doesn't just stop there. If they don't initiate a review you need to create an opportunity for the client to give you feedback – and for you both to redesign the alliance if necessary.

In fact, you should encourage them to do so even if their first reaction is to say everything's fine. For one thing it allows you to improve what you do. For another you become a role model for your client of being willing to continually learn and adapt what you do to get a better result.

This doesn't mean having a review at the end of every session – although some coaches may choose to do this. It's essential to review how things are going at the half-way stage – usually at the end of session three. If you want to make sure you get specific feedback you can ask your client to focus on a particular aspect of your coaching as well as giving a general overview.

It's a rare coaching relationship where there aren't a few problems to deal with – and not just with the clients. It's all too easy for the coach to jeopardize proceedings by allowing their own issues to get in the way. Chapter 16 discusses this in detail and provides an explanation of how to overcome obstacles and to make sure you don't contribute to your client's problems.

Logistical issues

It's essential, for your own benefit and that of your clients, to handle the logistics of your coaching sessions well. Before each session you need to prepare – in a number of different ways.

The environment

Think carefully about the room where you coach. If you work from home or have an office you can be in full command of it, making sure there are some water and drinking glasses, and any stationery that might be needed, such as pens, paper and possibly a flipchart. If you're coaching at someone's office or an anonymous meeting room in a hotel somewhere, you'll have less control, and will need to take along anything you think you might need. Wherever the room is, try to ensure it's warm enough without being hot – you don't want your client nodding off, and make sure it's well ventilated for the same reason.

Prepare yourself

Before each session look back over any notes you made during or after previous meetings and reflect on the discussions you've had. When you've only got one client it's easy to remember all the details. When you've got a dozen or more on the go at once, and sometimes gaps of a month or more between sessions, you'll need your notes to make sure you're up to speed with their issues. The pre-coaching questionnaire can also provide a useful refresher on the client's values, primary focus etc.

'How hard can it be just sitting and listening to people all day, and asking questions?' Well, it may appear easy, and even relaxing, but coaching can be extremely draining if you're putting your all into it. The reality is that by the end of a lengthy period of coaching your energy levels may be low. When you're working as a coach you have a responsibility to your clients to behave in a professional manner. This means you need to make sure you're in a good physical and mental state.

Executive Coaches can find themselves coaching for several hours at a time or even a whole day. In these circumstances it's useful to schedule breaks because long sessions can be tiring for each party and, of course, you and your clients will need the odd comfort break.

A few simple tricks will help you stay on top form:

- Drink water regularly so you don't dehydrate and lose your mental sharpness.
- Eat throughout the day to replenish your energy levels.
- Do a few stretching exercises to energize your body.
- Spend five minutes between sessions meditating or visualizing to recharge your battery and restore your mental state.
- Get some sleep so that you are fresh and rested – don't stay up late the night before as you won't be at your best.

What you can do

- Create a well-formed outcome for one of your own goals so you have a good idea of how the process works.
- Practise breaking large goals down into smaller goals.
- Pay attention to your own gremlins to make it easier to spot those of your clients.
- Set clients homework assignments that fit their issues.

12

questioning and listening

In this chapter you will learn:

- about questions
- that not all questions are equal
- the importance of listening
- different styles and levels of listening
- the power of silence.

The importance of listening

It's often said that we have two ears and one mouth – which should be used in that proportion. That's a good rule for everyday conversations. But it's not true of coaching. Unless you offer some kind of specialist service – Internet, Wealth, Lifestyle coach etc. – which is as much mentoring and training as it is coaching, talking for one-third of the time is way too much. That would be 20 minutes in a one-hour session, which we would regard as excessive. Most effective coaches listen a lot and only speak a little. They're committed to devoting as much time as possible to the client, creating a space in which they can clarify their thoughts. Out of that hour we suggest you limit yourself to no more than 12 minutes – that is 20 per cent – and less if possible. You can see now why we said earlier that coaching is not like having a normal chat with a friend.

Questions are the answer

'Questions are the answer'
Anthony Robbins, *Awaken the Giant Within.*

At the heart of coaching lies the skilful use of questions. They're an essential part of your toolkit and the principle way you support your clients in finding out more about their issues. While there are obviously many other facets to coaching, much of each session will usually be devoted to asking questions and listening carefully to the responses.

Now, you may already know a lot about questions and could be tempted to skip this chapter or just skim through it. They're covered on just about every management course and you may even have discussed the difference between Open and Closed questions when you were at school or college. But you can never know too much about this vital area – and there's more to it than meets the eye. We'll be looking in detail at when and how to use various types of questions.

The purpose of asking questions

The musician Brian Eno once said that the reason people have conversations is to find out what they think. And that's the primary purpose of asking questions during coaching. To be able to answer your questions your client needs to access, organize and articulate their thoughts. This promotes awareness – which is the first step towards having more choice and making a change.

Often, as they respond to your questions, people discover thoughts, beliefs, opinions, values and ideas they didn't know they had. Sometimes people are astonished when they bring to awareness information that had previously been unconscious. We all can, and do, believe things that don't make sense. And it's only when they're dredged from the darkest depths of our being and exposed to the cold light of day we realize how irrational they sometimes are.

Probing, powerful questions take clients deeper into their own experience, and reveal aspects of themselves which they didn't know about. One of the first things you need to do when working with a client on an issue is to help them understand it better. Occasionally this is all that's necessary for the person to be able to resolve it. They know what to do and how to do it – and the problem disappears.

Curiosity is the key

The key to asking useful questions is curiosity. When you're genuinely interested in the other person you'll want to know as much as possible about what's going on for them – and it will be easy to come up with a stream of inquiries. Curiosity is an essential mindset. A way of approaching the whole art of coaching. When you're curious you wonder what's going on for your client. What lies at the heart of the behaviour and beliefs they're describing? It's also easy to get carried away on a tide of curiosity so you need to temper it and not get too caught up in their story.

All questions are not equal

Rookie newspaper reporters are told on their very first day that there are five key questions they need to cover in any story: Who?, What?, Why?, Where? and When? These are often summed up in the opening paragraph of an article:

> Last month John Smith cycled from Land's End to John O'Groats to raise money for charity.

The interview that led to the story might have gone something like this:

John Smith   (*calling on the telephone*): Hi, I wonder if you'd like to do a write-up on something I've just done?
Reporter: Don't know. **What** was it?
JS: I recently cycled 1350 kilometres.
Reporter: Wow! From **where** to where?
JS: From Land's End to John O'Groats.
Reporter: Sounds interesting. **Why** did you do that?
JS: To raise money for charity.
Reporter: **When** did you do it?
JS: Last month.
Reporter: **Who** did you say you are?
JS: John Smith.

Given the effectiveness of these five questions in getting to the heart of the story you might imagine you'd use the same set in coaching. But one you should avoid, or at least use carefully, is 'why?'– because it can often sound like criticism. The question 'Why did you leave your wife?' is likely to lead to self-justification and defensiveness, while the question 'What was going on for you when you left your wife?' allows the client to explain their perspective.

You should also take care with 'How?' because it evokes analytical, conscious mind thinking, and often the problem – and solution – lie at the unconscious level. Rather than 'How do you plan to resolve this issue?', try 'What needs to happen for this issue to be resolved?'. They may sound identical, but the way the mind works in responding to them is different.

Asking the 'wrong' question

At any point in a coaching session there are literally dozens of different questions you could ask – many of which would take the discussion in an entirely different direction. How do you decide where to go?

It's a bit like playing chess. One move opens up the option of certain future moves but closes down the possibility for others. What if you get it wrong and opportunities are lost forever?

Well, as far as we're concerned – and this will reassure many experienced coaches as well as those just starting out – there really is no 'right' or 'wrong' question. Everything you ask will elicit a response of some kind. If your question doesn't connect with your client they'll either say so or struggle to answer it – and then you ask another. 'Mistakes' are rarely terminal, and can sometimes take the conversation in an unexpected but valuable direction.

When your mind goes blank

Sometimes when you're coaching your mind goes blank. It can happen even when you're a veteran, not just during your first sessions. You have no idea what to ask or say next. What do you do? Well, the best option is to have a number of simple, stock questions you can use in just about any situation, while you gather your thoughts such as:

- Where do think this is going?
- How do you feel about that?
- What's the real issue here?

By the time the client has answered you should be in a position to continue the session with confidence.

Open and closed questions

Since the aim of coaching is to empower clients, and to follow their agenda, it's best whenever possible to ask 'Open' questions, which allow them to move in the direction that's important to them. The more 'Closed' and focused the question, the more you are following your own thread. Another advantage of open questions is that they elicit a lot more information. They encourage the person to explore issues. Closed questions invite a one word answer – often 'yes' or 'no' – and that's one of the reasons why they should be avoided.

Sample dialogues

Closed: Is the issue here delegation?
Client: No.

Open: What's the issue here?
Client: I'm not sure. It could be a number of things. (Pauses) It feels like there's more work than there are hours in the day. Maybe I need to use my time better. (Pauses) Or perhaps I could delegate more.

Closed: Is the next step to define your goal?
Client: Yes.

Open: What's the next step?
Client: Well I'm getting to the stage of wanting to decide what to do, but I'd like to explore the options a bit more first.

The funnel technique

When asking questions, the aim is generally to begin broadly and then to narrow in scope while still letting the client drive the direction of the discussion.

Sample dialogue

Coach: So how would you like to spend the time today?

Client: It's been a hell of a week at work. I'd like to look again at ways of doing something more fulfilling.

Coach: Where would you like to start?

Client: By considering whether setting up my own business might be an option.

Coach: You've had a chance to reflect on our discussion. What thoughts do you have now?

Client: I really want to go for it. I've got a great idea for producing bespoke, premium furniture.

Coach: What do you want to focus on?

Client: All I need is to find some finance. That's what I'd like to explore.

Clarifying, probing questions

Given that one of the key reasons for asking questions is to raise awareness, so the client understands better what's going on, it can be useful to follow lines of enquiry that clarify anything which is unclear. People are vague in what they say, and there can be gaps in your understanding. If you, as coach, are not sure about the situation it's possible your client won't be as well. Probing with precision questions can help recover information that's missing. This also stops you making assumptions about what the person is saying and going off in the wrong direction. Asking for more detail, and specifics, avoids that problem – as well as revealing faulty logic, limiting beliefs and confused thinking.

Sample dialogue

With assumption and lack of clarification

Coach: How are things?

Client: Well, I'm still not getting to the gym like I said I would.

Coach: What's stopping you finding the time?

Client: Well, it's not really about the time.

Coach: You're having problems with motivation then?

Client: No, that's not it either.

With clarification and without assumption

Coach: How are things?

Client: Well, I'm still not getting to the gym like I said I would.

Coach: What's stopping you?

Client: The guy I was planning to go with is away at the moment.

Powerful coaching questions

Probing, clarifying questions are also often powerful and profound – taking your client into a deeper understanding of their issue, allowing them to see things from a new perspective or giving them an insight that leads to action. You know when a question's been powerful because people often pause, and there may be a period of silence, while they process information.

Simple questions are often more powerful than complex ones. They're easier for people to process mentally, and seem to connect more easily. The 'dumbest' questions can be the most effective.

- What do you want?
- What stops you doing X?
- What would happen if you did?
- Now what?
- When will you do it?
- What's the real issue here?

However, a question is only powerful if it comes at the right moment – at another time it will have no impact at all.

One question at a time

It's also important not to string several questions together, because it can be difficult for the client to hold them all in their mind – with the result that you either get confusion or a superficial response.

Steve once had a coach who, having asked him one question had a tendency to follow up with another question, and sometimes two more. The first question would be something like: What's important to you here? To which she might add, How does it fit with your values?, and, additionally, In what way does it connect with your goals?

Steve found it difficult to answer. While each is an excellent question in its own right, stringing all three of them together just threw him into overload.

Questions can also be unnecessarily complex, and that can have the same effect. How would you answer the following question?

> If you were to think what it would be like if you still had this problem in two years' time, and you could avoid that by taking action now, what is it you would do and what, if any, support do you need?

Questions as statements

If you endlessly ask question after question it can start to seem to your clients as if you're interrogating them. So for variety, try using statements that imply a question – raising your voice at the end if necessary to indicate that you're asking for a response.

- That must have surprised you.
- You have come up with some interesting options.
- I wonder what's going on here.
- You don't seem very happy about that.

Summarizing

Another way of preventing a session turning into an interrogation is to summarize periodically. This helps ensure you have a clear and accurate understanding of what's been said. Standing back and reviewing can provide a welcome break – like setting up a 'base camp' when climbing. Following a series of questions about values, you might summarize like this:

> So, the most important thing right now is to honour your value of freedom – and that is being violated by the long hours you have to work. What you want to do is find a way of cutting back or even switching to another company where they are less demanding.

The client can then confirm or clarify your understanding, allowing you to move forward and ask further questions.

Questions are presuppositions

Keeping to your client's agenda and not 'leading the jury' is an ambition that's admirable, but it's actually very difficult, if not impossible, to achieve. That's because virtually every question you could think of includes one or more presuppositions. Take the seemingly innocent question, 'What do you want?' Here there is an assumption that the person does want something. And 'Who else is affected?' assumes other people are affected.

Often these presuppositions are valid, but it's good to be aware of them all the same, because sometimes they're not. Presuppositions can also be negative in nature. 'What's your problem?', assumes the client has a problem.

Using presuppositions to empower

This presuppositional facet to questioning can be used powerfully and deliberately to empower clients and orient them towards a positive outcome. Consider these questions:

- How are you going to resolve this issue?
- What resources do you have that can help?
- How will things be better once you've done this?

What presuppositions did you identify? There are quite a few of them, including:

- The issue can be resolved.
- The client is going to do it.
- The client has resources which can help.
- That it will be done.
- That things will be better.

Are these questions neutral? No. Do they take the client in a particular direction? Absolutely. Is that a bad thing? Well, it depends on your point of view. We believe such empowering questions support the person you're working with. Assuming they have resources, abilities and power can be a self-fulfilling prophecy.

Questions that focus attention

Most questions are asked to elicit information, but another function can be to focus attention. This forms the essence of the Inner Game approach. Rather than telling someone to keep their eye on the ball when learning tennis, the coach would ask them questions about the ball ('Which way is it spinning?', 'How high is it as it crosses the net?') which have the effect of focusing the person's attention on the ball, rather than the movement of the racket.

The same approach can be taken in many other areas, including getting rid of habits and improving skills and capabilities. If, for example, someone is working on becoming better at public speaking, you might ask questions that get them to focus on the audience ('Which people seem to be most responsive?') rather than on their own concerns about whether they're doing it right.

The art of listening

'In the flow state, action follows upon action according to an internal logic that seems to need no conscious intervention.'

Mihaly Csikszentmihayli

It goes without saying that it's a complete waste of time asking powerful questions if you don't listen carefully to the answers. Yet we've seen it happen. There can be a certain amount of 'stage fright', with coaches so keen to show off their skills and look good to their clients – and themselves – that they spend all their time focusing on the next thing they're going to say, rather than on the person.

So, as soon as possible, you need to get to the stage where you no longer have to 'think' or 'plan' what question you're going to ask next – when the moment comes you simply open your mouth and something comes out. Your aim is to be in a 'flow' state, where no internal dialogue gets in the way, and you can be fully attentive to what your client is saying.

Listening 'validates' the person being heard – it acknowledges that what they're saying is important and has value. This encourages them to say more, and accelerates the process of coaching. In her wonderful book *Time to Think* (1998), Nancy Kline says 'Listening of this calibre ignites the human mind. The quality of your attention determines the quality of other people's thinking.'

So don't just listen – show that you're listening. Let them be in no doubt. Turn your body towards them and lean slightly forward to show that you're interested in what they're saying.

Superficial and deeper listening

The importance of listening really can't be overstated. It's one of the key skills of coaching. Part of its value is that it's so rare in everyday life. Perhaps you've had the experience of hearing two people supposedly 'having a conversation' when in reality they were simply exchanging monologues, only listening at a superficial, 'cosmetic' level.

That won't do when you're coaching. To be effective you need to tune into what's happening at a deeper level, to listen in an 'active', 'focused' way. It's not just the words they say or even the expressions they use. It's how they say them and being aware of the emotional undertone. The voice gives much away to the keen, attentive listener – you can attend to variations in tone, pace and volume. What energy does your client place behind particular words? When and how do they indicate excitement, fear, enthusiasm or sadness about something.

You can go even deeper still by listening for what's not being said. What are they avoiding or ignoring at a conscious or unconscious level? By drawing attention to them you increase awareness – and open the door to change. Your antenna needs to be tuned for subtle nuances in the way your client expresses things.

Listen with your eyes as well

It's not just your ears you need to use when you're listening, it's your eyes as well – look at your client's body language and facial expressions. Are their hands fiddling with something imaginary, feet shuffling, and arms folded? Movements like these when taken together may indicate anxiety or resistance. Maybe they start leaning slightly towards you when a particular subject comes up – indicating that it's of particular importance to them. And look out for mismatches between what someone is saying and their expression.

Sample dialogue
Coach: How did the meeting go?
Client: Not very well, I'm afraid. I ended up arguing with the Production Manager again. (Smiles)
Coach: I notice you smiled when you talked it about.
Client: Well, yes, actually I quite like our little 'set-tos'.

When there's a mismatch between the verbal and non-verbal aspects of a communication, it's the non-verbal aspects which are normally telling the truth.

Practise listening

Like coaching itself, listening is a natural skill, but one that most people have never actively developed. It is, however, something that can be improved considerably with practise. The easiest way is to listen to the radio – tuning in to a station where there's lots of chat. Then just listen carefully, without trying to focus on anything in particular. What do you notice? Over a period of time you may observe certain patterns. Perhaps the voice gets faster or louder when the person is agitated. Or has a mellow quality when they're remembering something that moved them. The more you practise listening the more discernment you'll have when working with a client.

Barriers to effective listening

One thing that can prevent you listening as well as you might is when you are worrying about what you are going to say next. Do this in a coaching session and your client will soon notice and may come to the conclusion that you're not interested in what they have to say. It's also all too easy to get sucked in by the first part of what someone says, make a connection to something you already know, and then put two and two together and make five. Try to avoid jumping to conclusions based on their opening remarks. Wait until you have all the facts. Racing ahead is not only irritating for others but a recipe for misunderstanding what they're trying to communicate. It can be a challenge to wait for someone who's rather long-winded, but if you cut them short you may miss something important.

Intuition – beyond listening

Some experienced coaches go beyond just listening. It's as if they enter some kind of 'zone' that allows them to pick up what's being communicated at an even deeper level. They just have a sense of something – are able to tap into their intuition – and trust that what they come up with may have value. It may be an idea of where to go, what to do next, what direction to follow. Sometimes it's a thought, image or question that just pops into their head.

Whether intuition comes – as some believe – from 'out there', or is simple information that's been stored unconsciously, experience has shown that it can often be right. So when you get a gut feeling or hunch it's important to honour it. Sometimes it will connect. At other times it will be off the mark. The critical thing is to not only let your client know about your insight but let go of it being the right answer to their issue.

Sample dialogue

Client: I'm not sure if I want to be part of this group. It seems to be yet another thing that's spreading me too thin. I seem to have so many things to juggle already but if I let it go I feel I'll be letting those people down. They seem to rely on me.

Coach: Your business is doing well and you're good at juggling. What does it mean to let them down?

Client: Part of what I want to do is to help people develop and grow. If I leave the group it will be like abdication. I don't think I'm indispensable or anything like that but I do feel I will have let them down in some way. (Voice trails off giving the impression of sadness or disappointment).

Coach: I sense that you feel sad when you think about this, and perhaps there's more to this for you.

Client: (Pause) I feel sad because I think in some way that if I continue with the group I'll be letting me down. I'm important in the same way that they are important.

Coach: What do you want to do about this?

Client: Take action. I guess I've been ignoring it, hoping it will go away. They'll manage well enough without me and I can find less time-consuming ways to support them. I will pull out of the group.

The power of silence

Just because your client has stopped talking it doesn't mean they've stopped thinking. One of the most important things you can do is to resist the urge to jump in and ask another question.

This is not a 'conversation'. This is coaching. Pauses create space for the other person to think more deeply. Often it's a sign that they're exploring new inner territory. Wait. And then wait some more. Clients will often go deeper and discover a lot of new things or say something that's revealing.

Yin and yang

Questioning and listening are the yin and yang of effective coaching. If you want to become a great coach these are the arts you need to master most.

Knowing when to stay silent and hold your peace is as important as knowing when to go in with a challenging and truly powerful question.

What you can do

- Become more aware of how good you are at listening by seeking feedback from people who know you well.
- Turn listening into a game and take every opportunity to actively listen out for not only what is said but also for the underpinning emotions.
- Recall a time when you were really curious about something then, from this mindset, start to practise asking questions
- The next time you're in conversation with someone, find an opportunity to ask them a presupposition question that will empower them in some way.

13

powerful tools and techniques

In this chapter you will learn:
- how to apply and use a range of tools and techniques
- how to expand your range of coaching skills.

Ways to facilitate change

While asking questions and listening will be at the heart of what you do as a coach, there will be times when it is appropriate to introduce a tool or technique that stretches your client and takes their thinking in a new direction. Occasionally, you will plan to use these tools ahead of time, but more often than not it may occur to you during the session that this is the right intervention to make. This chapter is full of empowering ideas that facilitate change.

Tolerations

What are you putting up with in your life right now? What frustrations and irritations are you tolerating? Perhaps you're accepting a less than satisfactory relationship because you can't face the thought of living on your own. It could be you're holding off buying a new bed because money's so tight. Or maybe it's something as trivial as a toilet seat that's needed fixing for the best part of five years.

Tolerating things such as unmet needs, difficult people, unfinished business and sometimes our own behaviour drains our energy and drags our spirits down. But over time we can get so used to them we barely even notice they exist – they may even become something we think we have to live with. But we don't have to – and neither do our clients.

Dealing with tolerations is a central focus for graduates of the CoachVille and CoachU schools of coaching – two of the best known American organizations for providing coaching training. They will normally ask their clients in the first session to list as many things as they can think of that they're putting up with. Sometimes they struggle at the start and then before you know it they have a list as long as your arm. Then they ask if there are any that can be 'zapped' immediately. There's usually one and sometimes more. It could be something like asking a spouse to check in with you before switching TV channels or simply tidying up a pile of papers.

Eliminating tolerations leaves people feeling energized. It gives them more time and makes it possible to move forward more quickly. The late Thomas Leonard, who started CoachU and CoachVille, urged his clients to reduce their tolerations by at least 90 per cent – and in the process take back control of their lives.

Using structures to create habits

Human beings are creatures of habit. We do a lot of things on 'auto pilot'. We have a routine. We get up, shower, take breakfast, brush our teeth and go out the door – often without conscious thought. We drive to our place of work in the same way. And if we're not careful we can 'sleep-walk' through much of the day.

Mostly we don't choose our habits deliberately. We sort of develop them in a haphazard, random fashion. Some people come to coaching because they have habits they want to lose, such as drinking too much or worrying. Others have habits they would like to 'install', such as eating healthily or having a positive mental attitude.

Creating new habits is relatively easy. One simple but effective technique is to suggest to clients that they introduce 'structures' to focus their attention on what they want – which helps to keep them on track. They could be as specific as doing ten minutes of salsa practice every morning or as general as putting a Post-It note on the fridge to counter emotional eating.

Opinions vary on how long you need to do something before it becomes a habit. Some psychologists say it takes 21 days. Others suggest longer and shorter time scales. In our experience it depends on the individual and the situation. But if your client sticks with it, sooner or later it will become so much part of their routine they don't have to think about it any more.

Sample dialogue

Client: I want to get fit but weeks go by and all my good intentions of going to the gym come to nothing.

Coach: Maybe you could create a routine or habit using structures (Explains briefly how these work). What do you think you could do?

Client: Hmm. I think one problem is that I could go to the gym at any time, so at the end of a hard day I say to myself 'I'll go tomorrow instead'. Then I do the same the next day. Perhaps if I signed up for a particular class, such as circuit training, I'd have a reason to go at least once a week. I'd need to ring-fence that commitment though.

Coach: Sounds good. Anything else?

Client: Well (Thinks) I could put my trainers in the car and drop into the gym straight after work. Once I get home I tend to become a couch potato.

Coach: Neat idea. Any other thoughts?

Client: Just one. I've got a colleague who's also a member. Maybe we could 'buddy up' and go together. We could agree a regular night once a week.

Creative visualization

Creative visualization is 'the art of using mental imagery and affirmation to produce positive changes in your life' (Gawain, 2002) – so the value it brings to coaching is obvious. Most of the people we work with are looking to improve their lot, and this is a powerful tool that can help them do that.

It also couldn't be easier. All your client has to do is imagine in as much detail as possible how they would like things to be. If they want to be able to chat more confidently to people of the opposite sex they simply create a movie in their mind of them doing so – and play it as often as possible. Although it's known as visualization, it doesn't matter whether or not your client can actually conjure up mental images. Some people just have a sense that it's going on but don't actually see it. It's a bit like day-dreaming, but with a specific purpose – and that can be a good way of describing the experience to your clients.

How does visualization bring about change? By programming the unconscious mind. Thoughts are powerful things. Where our attention – and intention – goes, energy flows. The brain can't differentiate between something that's remembered and something we've imagined, because they both use the same neural pathways. So when in the future we find ourselves in a particular situation, and check back on how we handled it in the past, we find what appears to be a positive memory that was in reality a visualization.

Once you've explained the technique to your clients they can do it whenever they want – and with as many issues as they like.

Using metaphor

When you're working with clients you'll often hear them talk about aspects of their life in metaphorical terms: 'I'm juggling frantically at the moment', 'My life is like a bottle of lemonade that's gone flat', 'I've got a knot in my stomach'.

These descriptions may sound arbitrary or accidental, but in fact they're an accurate representation of how the person is experiencing the situation. That's because symbolism is the natural language of the unconscious mind.

What's all this got to do with coaching? Well, if you want to engage with your client you need to get beneath the surface of their communication and explore their issues at a deeper level. Working with their metaphors can enable you to do just that.

> Amanda had a client who described herself as being surrounded by glass. It protected her from the world and kept her safe – yet separated her from the life she wanted to lead. It seemed to impede communication too. During the coaching session she decided the glass no longer needed to be there. The next day she called Amanda unexpectedly to say she'd been walking down the street and was aware of feeling different – 'sort of free'. She was delighted and curious about the change she'd made.

When you first work with your client's metaphors it can feel a little strange – as if you're 'stepping into a strange world' (there's another metaphor!). To coach effectively you need to be curious in your questioning and comfortable with ambiguity. Just accept and acknowledge their experience without trying to change it and then work with them in exploring it using 'clean' – or not contaminated with your own agenda – and open questions.

Sample dialogue

Client: It feels like I'm on a fairground ride.
Coach: What kind of ride?
Client: It's a merry-go-round with lots of bright colours and poles going up and down.
Coach: What can you tell me about it?
Client: It feels out of control.
Coach: Out of control?
Client: Yes – it's spinning way too fast for me to take anything in.
Coach: How do you feel about that?
Client: It makes me dizzy. I can't seem to focus on anything.

If you want to know more about working with metaphors, the books *Metaphors in Mind* (2002) by James Lawley and Penny Tompkins and *Metaphoria* (2002) by Rubin Battino may be of interest to you.

Increasing choice

Often when clients have problems it's because they only have one choice in a particular situation. Someone's coming round to their house and they must have it spotless. A colleague criticizes them and they feel the need to criticize back. Whenever there's a 'need', a 'must' or a 'should' there's no choice. People who behave in this way are like Pavlov's dogs, who have been conditioned to salivate when they hear a bell ring.

One of the ways you can support your clients is by drawing to their attention times when you observe them having limited choice. And if it seems relevant to the issue they're working on, encourage them to come up with other options.

Sample dialogue

Client: I get angry when people are late for meetings.

Coach: What do you do?

Client: Well, nothing really. What's the point?

Coach: Is that how you always handle it?

Client: Pretty much. I just sit there fuming. I don't say anything.

Coach: But you don't seem very happy. It seems like you only have one way of responding in this situation. Is there nothing else you could do?

Client: I suppose I could be more laid back about it. It doesn't seem to bother most other people.

Coach: I have a sense that wouldn't work for you.

Client: Too right! They should be on time. It's just not acceptable.

Coach: So can you think of any other options? What other choices do you have?

Client: I guess I could be more assertive and say I'm not happy. At least they'll know how I feel and they might do something about it.

'Experiments' and 'failure'

How do you encourage and support clients who say they want to change but never do anything different because they're afraid to get out of their comfort zone? What can you do to translate all the talking into doing? It's only when people push beyond what they perceive their boundaries to be that growth and learning occur. One concept that can work with some clients derives from Gestalt Therapy – the 'experiment'. People are often open to the idea of trying out a new behaviour – or even a completely new belief – when they know they're not making a commitment they can't go back on. It's just an experiment. If it doesn't work they can simply revert to where they were before. In some situations they might even carry out a range of experiments, to find out which gives them the best results.

One option is to suggest the client experiments with a change as homework – with a review the next session.

Sample dialogue

Coach: How are you doing with that issue of holding back and not really contributing in meetings?

Client: No change there, I'm afraid. It's still work in progress.

Coach: Have you got any meetings this week?

Client: Yes, there's one on Wednesday and another on Thursday.

Coach: Would you be willing to try an experiment, with no commitment on your part?

Client: Maybe. What is it?

Coach: Well I wonder if you'd be willing at one of those meetings to see what happens when you put forward an idea. You could prepare ahead of time if you'd feel more comfortable with that.

Client: I don't know. I guess no harm could come of it. If it doesn't work out I don't have to do it again?

Coach: That's right. Let's talk about what happens in the next session.

Some people embrace the idea of experiments but then don't actually do anything different. What often holds them back is fear of failure. Because they don't want to get it wrong they avoid taking risks and trying something new. If that's true of your client it can be valuable discussing the NLP presupposition 'There's no such thing as failure, only feedback' with them. This can be a liberating perspective when you fully take it on board. What would you be willing to try if you knew you couldn't fail? Pretty much anything!

We spend our childhood endlessly learning – how to walk, how to talk, how to write and so on. And we do it pretty much by trial and error. We have a go, make a start, and then learn from our mistakes. Using this 'feedback loop' we steadily improve, and keep on going till we crack it.

By the time we become adults, though, we often think we have to 'get it right first time'. We don't go skiing because we might fall over. We don't speak in public because we might screw up.

When you're coaching someone you'll often be supporting clients in taking risks. Knowing they can't fail and that everything can be just an experiment can allow them to step confidently outside their comfort zone. As Franklin D. Roosevelt famously said: 'We have nothing to fear but fear itself'.

Exploring multiple perspectives

One of the key benefits of coaching is that it expands the client's awareness. This can be about themself, other people, the world at large or even the nature of reality. Often they have information stored at an unconscious level that it would be useful to bring to the surface. A great way of doing that is by using the Perceptual Positions technique, which derives from NLP (Neuro-Linguistic Programming). There are three principal perspectives you can get your clients to explore – their own (first position), that of another person in the situation (second position) and that of a detached observer (third position). Most people are familiar with their own position, since they are in it most of the time. But getting your client mentally to 'step into someone else's shoes' and 'take second position' can be extremely enlightening for them. Not only do they harvest a surprising amount of information they were previously unaware of, they also get to see themself as the other person does. This can be especially useful in circumstances where there's conflict or your client wants to improve a relationship.

Sample dialogue

Client: I don't know what to do about one of the guys on the management team. He disagrees with everything I suggest and argues with anything I say. He's driving me crazy.

Coach: What do you think that's all about?

Client: I really don't know – he's just so in my face all the time.

Coach: Have you explored the situation from his perspective?

Client: No – and I'm not sure I want to!

Coach: (Laughs) I can understand that, but give it a go and see what happens.

Client: All right, if you say so!

Coach: Okay. Now just imagine being him for a moment, really get into his skin, and play a movie in your mind of the two of you arguing, but from his point of view.

Client: (Goes quiet and concentrates) Wow!

Coach: What did you see?

Client: Well – I don't quite know how to say this – but I can't
          believe how argumentative I'm being. It's as if I can't
          wait to shoot his ideas down in flames. And I look so
          smug when I'm doing it!

Asking your client to then take a detached, 'third' position,
often yields further insight because it places them outside the
communication process and their emotions don't get involved.

Sample dialogue

Coach: Now imagine you're a fly on the wall watching you and
          him fight.

Client: Okay. I'll give it a go. (Concentrates on his mind movie
          once again) Hmm. That is interesting.

Coach: What is?

Client: Well (Laughs), we're like two little boys in the
          playground arguing over whose Dad earns the most or
          whose got the best toys.

Coach: And?

Client: And it is all rather childish. I think it's time we both
          grew up. (Pause) I think it's time I grew up.

Sorting twisted thinking

While most of us consider ourselves to be rational, intelligent
people, the reality is often far from that. We can, and do, hold
all sorts of beliefs and have all kinds of thoughts which, when
we look at them objectively in the cold light of day are
obviously irrational and distorted.

One of the most powerful tools for dealing with 'twisted
thinking' of this kind is Cognitive Behavioural Therapy (CBT).
Since its development by Aaron Beck in the 1970s, CBT has
been adopted by many psychotherapists as one of the most
effective ways of dealing with everything from Obsessive
Compulsive Disorder (OCD), lack of confidence, to handling
emotions more effectively. More recently, a model of coaching
based on CBT has been developed. Cognitive Behavioural
Coaching uses the same principles as its therapeutic predecessor,
but it is more explicitly formulated around the use of questions
rather than direct intervention. At the heart of the Cognitive-
Behavioural approach is the ABC model, where:

• **A** is an **Activating event**, which may be external (the boss tells
  us that a piece of work we did is below standard) or internal

(we remember the boss telling us our work is below standard or we imagine the boss telling us our work is below standard).

- **B** is the Beliefs or thoughts we have about this – 'The boss thinks I'm no good at my job – he's going to fire me'.

- **C** is the emotional and behavioural Consequences that result – we feel down and depressed and perhaps eat a packet of biscuits or have an alcoholic drink.

It's commonly accepted in most cultures that external events, such as other people's behaviour, cause emotions. The language we use reflects that. We say 'he made me angry', 'the test is worrying me', 'that idea is getting me excited'. But the ABC model demonstrates that it's the thoughts we have and the beliefs we hold about those events that determine how we feel.

Most clients, when you explain this to them, experience a sense of regaining power. They're no longer victims of their emotions – they're in control of them. Instead of jumping to conclusions when the boss criticizes their work, they 'take it on the chin', admitting it was a bit sloppy and resolving to spend longer on it next time.

Every negative feeling results from a negative thought. Alter the thought and the emotion shifts as well. The key to bringing about positive change is to become aware of the Automatic Negative Thoughts (ANTs) you have. These systematically distort your experience of reality. Aaron Beck, who developed Cognitive Behaviour Therapy, came up with a detailed list of distortions. Working through it with your clients can enable them to discover how they create their own problems. Once they've identified the distortion they can do something about it.

Cognitive distortions

- **All-or-nothing thinking** – seeing things in terms of black and white; assisting the client in exploring shades of grey will help with this.

- **Magnification or minimization** – this is where the person exaggerates the negative and reduces the positive; what is needed is a sense of proportion.

- **Catastrophizing** – always assuming the worst; instead of focusing on possible results, ask the client to consider alternative outcomes.

- **Emotional reasoning** – this is where a person feels something strongly and assumes that this makes it a fact, 'I feel stupid therefore I must be an idiot'. Draw their attention to the flaw in their thinking.

- **Personalization** – the client blames themself for something that has happened even if it was not entirely down to them; once again a sense of proportion is required.

- **Shoulds, oughts and musts** – where the client criticizes themself or demands they follow self-imposed rules; more flexibility is needed.

- **Labelling** – the client attaches a meaning to a mistake or shortcoming transforming it into an identity statement such as 'I failed my driving test, I'm a useless driver'. Separate the behaviour from them as a person.

- **Mind-reading** – the client has negative thoughts and imagines these thoughts must also be in the minds of other people; the answer is to ask the other person what they think instead of guessing or assuming).

- **Fortune-telling** – the client believes things will work out badly: 'This is going to be tough' or 'it won't work out'. Encourage them to consider positive alternatives.

- **Mental filter** – The client dwells only on a negative aspect of a situation. Instead ask them to stand back and take a more balanced perspective.

- **Over-generalization** – The client makes assertions such as 'He'll never love me' or 'She always gets it wrong'. Statements like these don't take account of the times when the opposite is true. Challenge words like 'never' and 'always' – this will uncover the exception to their internal rule.

- **Discounting the positive** – The client ignores or completely disregards a more balanced view of things is required.

(Beck, 1976)

Acting as a mirror

One of the most valuable things you can do for your client is to act as a mirror for them, giving them feedback on any patterns of behaviour or thinking you observe. Everyone suffers from self-delusion to some degree and is unaware of their blind spots. As a coach you're one step removed from your client's experience, and able to notice things they miss.

When pointing out patterns, take care you don't come across as critical or judgemental. Think carefully about what you say and how you say it, and the likely impact it will have on your client. Honest feedback is one of the most precious gifts you can give, but it needs to be delivered with compassion and understanding if it's to be taken on board. If you're not sure your client is in the right 'space' ask them first: 'Would you be interested in hearing about something I've observed?' That gives them the opportunity to say no and provides a check to prevent you following your own thread rather than theirs. Here are some examples of the kind of feedback you might give:

- 'I don't know if you're aware, but you seem to use the word "must" a lot.'

- 'I've noticed that on a number of occasions you've avoided doing things because of what other people have said.'

Giving effective feedback is also an essential management skill, and performance issues can often be dealt with in a coaching style. One of the problems with feedback is if it's experienced as negative it can be counter-productive. You're looking to help build the person up not knock them down. So focus on ways of improving things in the future rather than raking over what went wrong in the past:

- **Be specific** – give examples rather than general comments.
- **Make it factual** – stick to what you actually saw or heard, don't confuse the issue with speculation.
- **Deliver it with empathy** – and with understanding.
- **Make it constructive** – it's only useful if the client can do something about it.
- **Focus on behaviour not identity** – 'You could have handled that better' rather than 'you're hopeless at handling things'.

What you can do

- Experiment with some of the tools and techniques in this chapter, starting by using yourself as a guinea pig. It's a good idea to have some personal experience to draw on:
  - keep a note of new habits you want to 'install'
  - start working through you personal list of tolerations
  - come up with a metaphor or symbol that represents the way you want to be as a coach.

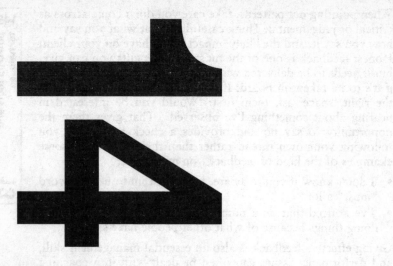

14

common themes and issues

In this chapter you will learn:
- about recurrent themes that arise in coaching
- tried and tested approaches to use with common coaching issues.

Recurring issues

It's often said that coaching's not 'remedial', that its purpose is to help people lead satisfying and fulfilling lives. That's the theory. But the reality, as any practising life coach will tell you, is very different. People often arrive with problems, which may be the reason they sought out coaching in the first place. And in a business context, coaches find themselves working with clients with specific issues they want to sort out.

While everyone you coach is unique, with issues and concerns that are personal to them, you'll find certain topics come up time and again. Exactly what you get depends upon whether you're doing corporate or life coaching – or a mixture of the two. But it's far from clear cut. Personal issues often come up when you're in a company, and matters relating to work are common in life coaching.

We've picked some recurring themes for discussion, to give you a 'head start' when they come up. But remember that you can never give any client an 'off-the-peg' solution. Skilled coaches offer bespoke solutions by digging beneath the client's presenting problem to discover and deal with deeper underpinning issues.

Procrastination

Many people fail to get round to doing things, put them off or give up soon after they've started. It's a problem known as procrastination – and it's extremely common. Sometimes it's so bad they seek out coaching to deal with it – perhaps because they recognize it's sabotaging their ability to achieve their goals and live their dreams. Other times it's hidden beneath issues that are more pressing as far as the client is concerned, and may not even feature in their Primary Focus. By the time you get to session two or three you're starting to get a glimpse of it. Each week the client reports not having done his or her 'homework'. Or they talk about issues they're having at work with tight or missed deadlines.

As with most problems there's no one cause and no one solution. You'll need to ask lots of questions to discover exactly how they're creating it. Try not to have any preconceived ideas. Keep an open mind or you risk putting them in a pigeon-hole that doesn't fit.

However, you'll find certain themes coming up time and gain. Often people with this pattern have a perfectionist streak. They see all the flaws in things which make tasks seem more challenging. Because they want to get it 'absolutely right', they take a long time doing them – especially when they consider them important. Sometimes they have a fear of failure or disapproval – which may operate out of conscious awareness – so they procrastinate to avoid criticism or feeling bad because things didn't work out as well as they hoped. Occasionally you'll discover that clients have a low tolerance of frustration. Because they think a task is going to be unpleasant or boring they're never in the mood to tackle it. And sometimes it seems so overwhelming they can't see the point in even starting.

Ways of dealing effectively with procrastination include:

- Encouraging the client to break large tasks down into smaller, more manageable chunks.
- Actually getting the client started, even if they don't know quite what to do.
- Asking the client to create structures and habits that make sure things move forward.
- Getting the client to become aware of their underlying beliefs about failure and success.

Be careful never to label the person a 'procrastinator', as this can compound the problem. Once they start thinking of themselves in that way it can become a self-fulfilling prophecy: 'Of course I put things off, that's just the way I am!'

When your client thinks they can achieve what the set out to do, they are likely to do just that.

Stress

Stress, like your clients, comes in all shapes and sizes – and chances are you'll see a fair bit of it in your coaching sessions. It's now cited as the commonest reason for time off work and the cause of a host of conditions from depression to diabetes. Many people complain of suffering from stress but the problem is they mean different things – because it's such a subjective experience.

Some find it stimulating to have lots of things on; others shut down because they start to go into overwhelm. Some seize up, like frightened rabbits in a car's headlights, when they have to sit in an interview; others savour the experience, enjoying the opportunity to 'show off'. Some are stressed by seemingly insignificant events and experiences; others take everything in their stride.

Stress is the reaction of the body to a perceived or present threat – stimulating the well-known 'flight or fight' response. In small doses it can act as a spur, boosting physical and mental well-being and helping people meet and overcome challenges. Too much stress, though, can take its toll – especially if it persists over long periods – leading to anxiety, exhaustion and sometimes health problems.

Typical stress situations include pressure, frustration, conflict and major life changes, such as divorce, moving house and switching jobs. If your clients report finding it hard to sleep at night, are suffering headaches or stomach upsets, or their blood pressure is up, they may have a problem with stress,

The secret to helping people deal with stress lies in finding out as much as possible about the problem – what situations evoke the response, when they occur, who else is involved etc. The more fully it's understood, the easier it is to do something about it.

As with many areas of coaching, once they bring their conscious attention to what was previously out of awareness many clients find it easy to make changes that reduce their stress levels. These may be physiological, such as exercising more and eating better, mental, such as not taking things so seriously, or practical, such as saying 'no' more often and delegating when that's an option.

Self-confidence and assertiveness

Some clients are only too aware they lack confidence, either generally or in certain situations. Others come to coaching with a different problem but after a session or two it becomes obvious to them and you that the underlying issue is really about poor self-esteem or a need to be more assertive. There's a difference between assertiveness, non-assertiveness and aggression that it can be useful to discuss with them.

- Assertive behaviour is 'I win – you win', with both parties expressing their feelings and thoughts openly and honestly while respecting each other's right to do so.
- Non-assertive behaviour is characterized by either not honestly expressing views, feelings and beliefs or doing so in an apologetic fashion. It's driven by a desire to avoid conflict,

be liked and wanting to keep the peace. It's 'you win – I lose'.

- Aggressive behaviour is intimidating, controlling, demanding and confrontational. It's about 'I win – you lose', and no one else is considered to be important. It's characterized by giving orders, shouting and interrupting.

When you're coaching a client who wants to behave more assertively you're probably dealing with a fear of some kind – such as a fear of hurting someone else's feelings or fearing rejection which results in attempts at winning approval. People sometimes value others over themselves or have a lack of self-worth and coaching can assist them in redressing the imbalance.

Work-life balance

Your clients are working longer hours than ever before. One in six is clocking up more than 60 hours a week, a third complain of headaches because of stress, and nearly half say they get irritable at home. Many get up at the crack of dawn to catch an early train or miss the commuter traffic, and as a result don't see much of their children or spouse during the week, struggle to get to the gym, and have little or no time for friends and other interests.

In a recent survey carried out by *Management Today* (2002), 76 per cent of managers say they want to spend more time with their families; 50 per cent report feeling mentally and physically exhausted; and 30 per cent say their lives are out of control. Success at work can, it seems, lead to failure in other areas of our lives – and that has a knock-on effect at work. It's a vicious circle.

No wonder, then, that work-life balance issues come up regularly for both life and executive coaches. Fitting everything they want into an already packed schedule can feel like a real challenge for your clients – and they'll be looking to you to help them improve things. What are you going to do?

As always, you need to start by finding out what's actually going on for them and not assume anything. Everyone has a different sense of what it means to be out of balance. What does it mean for your client?

Establishing clear, detailed outcomes can be extremely powerful and effective. How exactly will things be when their life is in balance? What steps can they take that will move them forward?

Time management

Sometimes the way to deal with work-life balance issues is to look with your client at their time management. Not everyone is efficient in this area, and a few small changes can make a big difference in the amount of time they have available to them.

You might suggest they keep a log of what they do throughout a day – or even a week. Clients are often surprised by the results, and immediately see ways in which they can save time. In any one week there are 168 hours available. Get them to add up how much time they spend doing various things. That can often be a revelation as well. People often realize there's a discrepancy between what's important to them and how they allocate their time.

The way people use their time often suggests they think they're going to live for ever. But there's a finite amount of time for each of us. If they live to be 75, the average age for men and women, they have, from the moment they're born, around 657,000 hours available to them.

> Jenny is a busy person who manages to cram a lot into her life, but when she added it all up she was amazed at how little time she had left. Working, sleeping, eating, travelling, shopping and washing together added up to around 120 hours – and that was without allowing time to be with her partner or children, going to the gym, seeing friends, watching TV, listening to music, or just chilling with a glass of wine and a good book. It was immediately obvious to her that she was 'doing too much', and she started to think realistically about what to let go and what to prioritize.

If your client is 30 now, they have somewhere in the region of 394,200 hours left. If they're 50 it may be no more than 219,000 hours. About a half that time will be spent sleeping, eating, washing and doing chores. Another chunk will be spent working.

The question is: How do they want to use this most precious of commodities?

One way you can assist your clients is by making sure that how they spend their time is congruent with their values and purpose in life. A great question you can ask is, 'How do you want to live your life?'

Leadership

'The most effective leaders are those who first learn to lead themselves.'

Jim Kouzes and Barry Posner,
The Leadership Challenge, 2003

Many clients in the business world hire a coach because they want to inspire their team, get buy-in to ideas, motivate people and align their efforts in achieving the company vision. They want to develop their leadership skills and be more effective, charismatic and dynamic. Such qualities are highly valued in the business community and essential for managers looking to make it to the top.

When you coach at this level you need to be prepared to challenge your clients. They will often be powerful, influential people who say what they think – and expect you to do the same. They don't necessarily get that degree of honesty and directness from their management team, so they're looking for a coach who's prepared to tell them the truth.

There are many excellent books on leadership – including *Principle-Centred Leadership* by Stephen Covey (1992) – and it's a good idea to read a few if this field is relatively new to you, so you have the latest thinking at your fingertips.

But it's easy to fall into the trap of thinking leadership isn't an issue in life coaching – that it's just about business. But personal leadership is also important. In fact, to be a good leader of others you need to be able to lead yourself. That means being clear about your purpose in life.

Real leadership is about being true to yourself, authentic even, with your behaviours aligned to your beliefs and values. People demonstrate this when they 'walk the talk' and practise what they preach. When you're coaching someone on the whole of their life it can be valuable to introduce the idea of personal leadership.

Delegation

Delegation is a big issue in business, and if you coach in-company or at executive level, you're bound to come across it. Many managers like the idea of letting go of some of the responsibilities but actually live by the creed 'If you want a job doing well do it yourself'.

What's going on here? Often they fear that if they don't personally supervise everything mistakes will be made because no one's as skilled as they are. So they keep a tight rein on every facet of the business.

One useful approach can be to look at the reality of the situation. Is there really nothing that could be safely delegated? It's normally possible – unless they're a complete control freak – to find a few things. Who in the team could they most trust to handle them? Once managers make a start on delegation they discover that many of their fears were unfounded.

When a client's experiencing problems with delegation it's useful to get them to second position their team. Once they realize how it affects others – and discover that it can be demotivating and demoralizing – they often make a commitment to alter their behaviour.

You might also focus their attention on how much more effective they'll be when they have delegated, and explore any other benefits, such as improved work-life balance and increased chance of promotion.

Happiness

'Don't worry, be happy,' sang Bobby McFerrin in the song of the same title. But many people find that easier said than done. In fact, a significant proportion of those who come to you for coaching will be unhappy in some way – and looking to change that situation.

So one useful thing you can do early in your relationship is to get your clients to rank themselves on a 'Happiness Scale' from 1 to 10 – similar to the Wheel of Life (see Chapter 8). You could even add it to the Wheel if you think it's a good idea. A score of 10 means 'I couldn't be happier'. A score of 1 means 'My life sucks'.

Wherever they are on the scale, most people would like to be happier. But what's going to achieve that? As with so many things, each person is different. Most commonly it is possessions, security, health, money, status, fulfilling employment, peace of mind, a soul mate, respect, exotic holidays and spiritual contentment.

So the coach's job should be easy. You find out what would make your client happy and help them achieve it. All done. But experience shows that it doesn't work quite like that. That's because happiness is, more than anything, a state of mind. It's an outlook. A way of thinking about things.

Consider this sentence: happinessisnowhere.

How did you read it? For some people it says 'happiness is nowhere. Others see 'happiness is now here'. Clever, eh? It's taken from Robert Holden's inspiring book *Happiness Now!* (1999) and shows how easily the same event can be interpreted in different ways. Happiness isn't determined by life circumstances. There are plenty of people who were born with a silver spoon in their mouth and have more money than they know what to do with who are as miserable as sin, while others who have lived through tremendous hardship or have nothing are as 'happy as Larry'.

Some clients will see the glass half empty, others half full. Some will focus on what's missing, and what they'd like to acquire, others will count their blessings and appreciate what they already have. Many people defer their happiness into the future. 'I'll be happy when I get a decent car/partner/job/house.' And that can lead to them being unhappy right now.

Effective ways of coaching people on happiness include encouraging them to be more in the present, identify their strengths and make use of them, and maintain a positive mental attitude.

Relationships

Relationships often find their way onto the coaching agenda. That's true whether you work with individuals or companies. You'll get clients who want to have satisfying, fulfilling relationships with other people and are finding it difficult because of conflict with family, colleagues or friends. Others will be looking for a soul mate, in a relationship that's going through a sticky patch, or getting over one that's failed.

Through questioning you will obviously want to explore what's going on. Here are the kinds of things you might ask:

- 'What precisely happens between you?'
- 'Which of your values are being violated?'

- 'What beliefs do you hold about the situation?'
- 'What part are you playing in this?'

The last question is particularly useful. We tend to think it's other people who create the problems in relationships but, as they say, it takes two to tango, and we have to own up to our responsibility as well.

Perceptual Positions is a great technique here because it produces so many new insights (see Chapter 13 'Exploring multiple perspectives'). Simply suggesting the client takes a look at the way they're behaving through the eyes of someone else can bring about a shift in their thinking and behaviour.

Money and finance

It's rare to do a 'Wheel of Life' with someone who's totally happy with their Money segment. Most people would like more of it – and some devote a significant proportion of their sessions working out how to get it.

Your clients are starting from various places of course. Some will be comfortably off and they will be looking for opportunities to increase their wealth. Others will be drowning under a river of debt – and wanting to find a way of keeping their head above water.

If you're not an experienced Money/Wealth coach, tread carefully when it comes to giving advice. There are certain areas of finance where specialist knowledge is required, and you should refer them to someone experienced in financial planning. But if all you're doing is asking questions to help the person build a solid monetary foundation that will be okay.

However, this segment can never be considered in isolation because it relates directly to so many of the others – most obviously work. But if there's not enough money it can affect relationships and health as well. And, ultimately, fun and recreation. Problems in the area of money can drag most of the other segments down.

One of the first things you could do with your client is carry out a 'reality check'. You need to know where you are starting from – even if things look bad. It might also be a good idea for your client to keep a money diary for a period – so you're both absolutely clear where the money's going. Follow that, perhaps, with a look at your client's spending habits. Do they impulse buy? Or are they careful with cash?

Setting a clear goal is probably the next step, whether that is to clear debts by a specified date or make it to a million in three years' time. Then it's simply a matter of creating a plan and putting it into practice.

Troublesome emotions

Everyone has trouble 'controlling' their emotions at some time – no matter how 'sorted' they are. We all get sad, angry, frustrated, impatient, hurt etc. Sometimes people want to deal explicitly with their emotions – perhaps through anger management – but even if that's not the case they often surface as an issue.

Most people believe they have no choice about the emotions they experience – and to some extent they're right. We're still driven to a surprising degree by primitive animal urges. We try to avoid these 'negative' emotions, because they can be inconvenient or even debilitating but they often have a purpose we're not aware of.

A client's anxiety about taking an exam may be telling them to prepare better. Asking them questions about the issue and their feelings will often allow them to get in touch with what's going on at a deeper level.

You may also find some of the ideas discussed in the last chapter on twisted thinking and the ABC model useful. You can ask your clients to note down the thoughts they're having that are creating the troublesome emotions. Once they've been brought out into the open they can be analysed and reviewed – and if it's appropriate, new choices can be made.

Spirituality

Coaching isn't just about goals and performance. Sometimes what we do is create a space where they can explore issues that are important to them. Increasingly this includes 'spirituality', with people searching to find meaning and purpose in their lives.

Note the small 's' and quote marks – spirituality is not necessarily about religion. It's about looking beyond the surface and getting in touch with the essence of who we are.

Aboodi Shabi, a highly regarded coach in the UK, specializes in coaching for the soul and he says: 'We might be performing well against measurable targets, or achieving our goals, but we might also be like empty shells, living lives that are automatic and soulless'.

When you coach someone who wants to develop their 'spiritual' side it helps to ask questions that stimulate their thinking about the legacy they want to leave behind them. Try asking them to imagine being on their deathbed looking back over their life. What is it they would like to have achieved? How would they like to be remembered?

There's nothing quite like a question of this kind to help clients put the small things in life in perspective and to sort the 'wheat from the chaff' when deciding how to live their lives.

What you can do

- Think about your own life and make a list of issues that apply to you and other people you know.
- Experiment with some of the ideas for facilitating change given in this chapter.
- Keep a log of themes you come across as you begin to coach your own clients.
- Note the similarities and differences between client issues and the ways you assist your clients in resolving them.

15 making things happen and raising the bar

In this chapter you will learn:
- how to create a climate that supports and stimulates change
- the energizing, motivating value of goal-setting
- the leverage that derives from accountability
- three powerful interventions that help people move forward
- how to monitor progress
- ways to encourage clients to achieve more than they believed was possible.

Coaching means change

Imagine you came to the end of a coaching relationship and your client was exactly the same as when you'd started. How would you feel? If a company sponsor was involved what would their perspective be? And what about the client? It's likely that everyone involved would consider it to have been a complete waste of time, effort and money.

The whole purpose of coaching is to bring about change – for the client to learn, to improve, to grow, to move forward in some way. From the outset of the coaching relationship your role as a coach is to create a climate that supports your clients in achieving their outcomes.

While this may still sound like a bit of a challenge right now, once you have expanded your understanding of processes such as goal-setting and accountability, and are familiar with interventions such as Requesting, Bottom Lining, Interrupting and Challenging, you will feel increasingly confident.

Stimulating change through goal-setting

In Chapter 11 we introduced you to the idea of goal-setting. Some of the people who come to you will already know what their goals are. Others may have reached a point in their life or career where they're unsure about what's important to them and where to go next. Becoming clear about their goals is sometimes all the kick start they need to make things happen.

Typically people will have a mix of short-, medium- and long-term objectives. Some will be quickly and easily accomplished – perhaps during the first week or two. Others will be more involved, and take longer. And some bigger issues last well beyond the coaching relationship.

But why have goals in the first place? Why not simply start coaching and see what happens? While that's certainly one approach – and precisely what some clients want – most people find that having specific, measurable outcomes provides direction and purpose, and with it a propulsion system in the form of motivation and energy. Simply having clearly articulated goals on its own stimulates change – because the client spends more time thinking about what they want and how to achieve it.

Accountability provides leverage

To be 'accountable', according to the *Collins English Dictionary*, is 'to be responsible to someone, or for some action' – and that is the common understanding of the word. If you say you'll be accountable for doing something, such as picking me up at 7.30pm that means you'll do it – and I have a right to complain if you don't.

While some coaches do take that approach it has significant disadvantages: few people respond well to the nagging of a strict parent or teacher figure, and the client isn't learning to take responsibility for themself.

Accountability, though, is at the heart of coaching, because it provides leverage that moves things forward. Many of us have items on our 'To Do' lists that have been there more years than they'd care to admit – and one of the reasons they've never been turned into reality is that they haven't 'gone public' with them.

When you make a commitment to another person you're more likely to follow through. However, it's important for clients to understand that completing an action is not about pleasing the coach. It's about doing something because it matters to them.

During the intake session an agreement is usually reached as to how the client wants the coach to hold them accountable. The most common arrangement is that the coach will ask in the next session about things the client said they were going to do – but offer inquiry and compassion rather than blame and judgement if things haven't been completed. This gives the client the opportunity to discuss with the coach what's going on without fear of retribution.

It's important for this to not feel like a 'witch hunt' because this will result in a defensive reaction. Coaching at its best is much more about peeling back layers of awareness than pushing to get things done. What you're aiming to do is objectively explore what went on. Sometimes if a person says they want to do something and they don't follow through it can be because they've changed their mind, didn't want to after all, it doesn't fit with their values, sense of self or higher purpose – it doesn't feel like them.

There needs to be, though, an expectation right from the start that clients will do what they say they will – otherwise you're letting them off the hook. Most clients start off completing tasks efficiently and enthusiastically, but after a while many will 'test' how 'strict' or 'lenient' you are when they haven't done their 'homework'. The best way of handling the situation is to ask them to review the accountability arrangements you've agreed. Once they realize they're not back at school, and the responsibility lies with them not you, this approach tends to foster greater self-reliance and growing independence.

This style of accountability can sometimes be difficult if you are in an organization and coaching a member of your staff. As a manager you have a right to expect certain things from your employees, and disciplinary procedures exist to deal with those who don't deliver. The problem comes when coaching gets mixed up with the legitimate requests you have to make of staff. It needs to be clear what's optional in the coaching relationship and what isn't.

161
making things happen
and raising the bar

15

The structure of accountability

To some extent, the structure of accountability drives coaching forward with three key questions that allow it to be tracked. What will you do? When will you do it? How will we know?

What will you do?
A goal without a deadline is just a dream. Adding a timescale for completion gives it weight, and makes accountability possible.

When will you do it?
A goal without a deadline is just a dream. Adding a timescale for completion gives it weight, and makes accountability possible.

How will we know?
This is the question that really allows accountability to be nailed down. Stating how specifically the coach and client will know the commitment has been met sets up a benchmark against which results can be judged.

Some clients have a tendency to be over-ambitious in the commitments they make, especially in regard to when they say they'll have them done by, and you may want to question them if you think they're being unrealistic.

Updates can be handled in as many ways as you can think of, including email, fax or voice mail, but many coaches begin their sessions with a review of progress since the last meeting – and this provides a good opportunity to check in on the things the client wanted to be held accountable for.

This sounds simple in theory – but it's not unusual for a client to launch straight into something that's happening for them and the moment is lost. It's important to follow their flow. If a chance to discuss accountabilities doesn't occur naturally during the conversation you'll sometimes be able to raise the topic towards the end of the session. This needs to be handled carefully. If your client has spent considerable time and effort doing something and you give it a cursory five minutes it can feel dismissive to them – and won't provide them with encouragement to follow through in the future.

Can you have a coaching relationship without accountability? The answer is an emphatic 'yes – but'. Some clients will ask not to be held accountable at all – or to be accountable only for specific things – and that is their prerogative. If your client is already very self-reliant, loves freedom or simply likes being in control, they're likely to feel constrained by accountability. Another situation you may come across is where the purpose of the coaching is less about getting something done and more about the person developing themself. Some clients may not feel the need for a coach to remind them of what they have said they'll do.

The downside of this approach is that it's much easier for clients to hide from issues they want to avoid or aren't ready to deal with.

Three key interventions that move things forward

There are three simple but powerful interventions you can use to assist clients to move forward:

1 Requesting action
2 Interrupting
3 Bottom-lining.

Requesting action

Directly asking your clients to make a commitment to taking action is one of the most effective ways of turbo-charging your coaching. Operating from an understanding of their agenda, and experience of them as a person, you ask them to do something which is specific and measurable – for which they will be accountable in whatever terms you have agreed.

The client has three choices:

1 To accept the request.
2 To decline the request.
3 To suggest an alternative.

Your responsibility as coach is to be willing to let go of the request if the person turns it down. What you thought might be useful for them obviously doesn't fit at this point in time. If you are genuinely operating out of the client's agenda, and not your own, you will find it easy to feel detached from your requests.

Presenting something clearly as a 'request for action' marks it out as significant – not just another thing you're asking of them – and as a result clients will often respond by saying 'yes'. The responsibility for doing it or not remains with them, but as they have made an unequivocal commitment they're more likely to see it through.

The request, though, must be specific and measurable if it's to move things forward. If what you ask is vague the results will be every bit as woolly. As the old saying goes, 'What gets measured gets done'.

If the client says 'no' to your request, you should ask them what they'll do instead. Often they will make some kind of 'counter-offer' which is more appropriate for them, and behind which they will be willing to put energy.

Sample dialogue

Client: I really don't want to have to catch up with work this weekend. I told some friends I'll visit them, and I can't let them down again.

Coach: I have a request to make. I would like you to commit to finishing all the work you need to do by Friday lunchtime, so you have time to start winding down.

Client: I don't think I could manage that, there's so much going on.

Coach: What will you commit to?

Client: I'll do an extra hour each night this week, and everything should be complete by 6pm on Friday.

Client: Sounds great. Enjoy your weekend!

Interrupting

While it might seem rude to interrupt clients when they're speaking, it's often valuable and occasionally necessary. They sometimes get so wrapped up in describing what's going on for them in such great detail that if you do nothing the session will be over with no progress made. During the intake session you will have told clients that you will sometimes interrupt them – to make best use of the time – so when you do they may be surprised for a moment, but will quickly understand why.

You can make it obvious what you're doing by actually using the word 'interrupt' – saying, for instance, 'Can I interrupt you a moment?'

Interrupting can be used at any time, but is often valuable in the following situations:

- When the client has wandered off the point, got distracted by a new thought, or gone off at a tangent.
- Where the client simply enjoys telling stories that seem to go on forever.
- When the client elaborates at length and discusses things in enormous detail.
- Where the client seems to be talking about inconsequential things as a way of avoiding discussing something they find hard to deal with.

As clients get used to you interrupting – hopefully not every time they open their mouth! – they'll quickly learn to be more concise when they're communicating, reducing the need for you to interrupt in the first place. Most of the time interruptions will be followed by another intervention, such as asking a question, offering feedback or requesting action – making your interruptions fit quite naturally into the coaching flow.

Sample dialogue

Client: Well, the thing about Dave is that he's not really a very good people manager. You'll never believe what he did the other day... (Starts telling a story similar to others from previous sessions about the same manager)

Coach: Can I interrupt you there? I'm interested in your story, and I also want to make sure you get the most out of the time we have together. What do you want to do to improve the situation?

Client: Well I could have a word with him, because his behaviour is affecting my team.

Bottom-lining

As an intervention bottom-lining has some affinity with interrupting, in that it's used when people start to ramble on, sometimes even losing track of the point they were trying to make themselves – but its purpose is different. If interrupting is like a stun grenade that stops your client in their tracks, bottom-lining is like a machete that allows you to cut through the jungle of their story and get to the heart of the matter.

Sometimes you may need to interrupt before bottom-lining, but in most coaching interactions you can use the technique simply by asking questions like this:

- What's the bottom line?
- What lies at the heart of this?
- What's the real issue?

These can be among the most powerful questions you can ask. You'll know you've 'hit the target' when the client goes quiet and spends some time thinking how to answer. You've taken them to a deeper level of awareness, and the understandings they develop as a result will often have a profound effect on the insights they have.

Another way of getting to the bottom line is to formulate a summary based on what they've said and feed it back to them. When you do this you need to make sure you check with them that you've really understood.

Sample dialogue

Client: (Speaks at some length)...and I just felt so let down and mad about the way he behaved. It was just so unfair of him to do that...

Coach: You were disappointed and angry. Is that right?

Monitoring progress

It's important to have some kind of mechanism by which you and your client can review the progress being made. First and foremost this allows both of you to establish that things are moving forward in a satisfactory way – so you don't get to the last session of an agreed programme only to realize nothing significant has happened. For the client, recognizing what has been achieved so far can also be a spur to further progress – encouraging them to set their sights higher, and sign up for objectives that are even more demanding.

Reviews can be scheduled so they happen on a regular basis, perhaps after every three or four sessions, or left to arise spontaneously. The advantage of planning them is they don't get forgotten – but this arrangement can feel too structured for some people, who prefer a more ad hoc approach.

One good way of kicking things off is to ask the client to reflect on where they are now in relation to where they started. They will almost certainly remember some of the main goals they set for the coaching relationship, and evaluate the progress they've made towards achieving them. You might also look back together at the objectives identified at the intake session, and 'tick off' those which have been completed – at the same time adding others which may have arisen since.

Sometimes clients aren't aware of the headway they've made in certain areas, and one of the most beneficial things a coach can do is draw attention to them. This allows the client to get a more accurate perspective on where they are now in relation to where they were when they started. This process can also be a good indicator for open-ended relationships when it's time for the coaching to end – because either there are no goals left or little further progress is being made.

Good questions for monitoring progress include:

• In what ways have things moved forward for you?
• Where are you now in relation to where you were when we started?

Raising the bar

When athletes are in training, with their hearts and minds set on winning an Olympic medal, their aim is constantly to improve on their best. And the way they – and their coaches – do that is by setting goals that stretch them – by regularly raising the bar to a higher level. Your clients are capable of more than they are currently achieving – often a lot more. Your role as coach is to help them maximize their potential.

Holding them big

'Holding them big' is a mindset that is valuable to have in relation to your clients. As you focus not on the person you see in front of you but on their potential instead, you give them confidence to take risks and dare to live their dreams – which in turn stimulates change and forwards the action. When you think in this way – that your client is 'up for something big' – they will sense you believe in them without you having to say it explicitly. What you hold to be true about people is evidenced in everything you do and say. Consider, for instance, these two questions:

- Do you think you'll be able to run that marathon?
- How will you feel when you've run that marathon?

The first implies you have doubts about your client's ability, while the second assumes they'll be able to do it. When you believe in your client you'll raise the stakes and support them in stretching further than they would otherwise.

Challenging

Challenging takes the requesting action intervention to the next level by 'daring' clients to move beyond their comfort zone. In requesting action, you are normally asking for something reasonable and attainable – but that is not the case with challenging. The primary purpose here is to 'raise the game' through shock value; your request must go beyond your client's belief of what they are capable of doing. If they blithely say, 'Okay, I'll do it,' without batting an eyelid, it isn't really a challenge.

So don't be surprised when they reject your challenge – in fact, it ought to be almost impossible for them to accept it. But what happens most of the time is that – once they've come back down from the ceiling – they'll make a counter-offer that's more of a stretch than if you'd simply made a request. This is a great way of raising the bar while still allowing the client to control the height at which it's set. What underpins Challenging is the 'Holding them big' mindset. As long as you make your request in a congruent way, really meaning it rather than being playful, the client will pick up on your belief in their potential, and their own sense of what's possible for them will be enhanced. Challenging is an intervention that should be used sparingly – spring it on your clients every session and it will lose its power.

Sample dialogue

You may find it useful to compare this dialogue with that from requesting action (p. 163).

Client: I really don't want to have to catch up with work this weekend. I told some friends I'll visit them, and I can't let them down again.

Coach: You've mentioned this before. Here's my challenge to you: Get everything that's important done by Thursday lunchtime and then take Friday off, so you have a long weekend with your friends.

Client: You're out of your mind! There's so much going on that it would be impossible.

Coach: What will you do?

Client: Well, with a bit of juggling and a couple of late nights on Tuesday and Wednesday, I could probably clear all the crucial stuff by early on Friday.

Coach: And?

Client: And that means I can take Friday afternoon off and go see my friends the same day.

Client: Sounds fantastic. Good thinking. Enjoy your weekend!

Striking the right balance

When you make any intervention that's designed to stretch your client it's important to make sure you don't push too hard. If you ask your client to do something when they're already overloaded it may be the straw that breaks the proverbial camel's back. There's no easy rule of thumb. It's a question of gauging where they're at. Some coaches do this naturally and easily others need to develop the skills. What lies at the heart of this is being aware of what's happening for them and how they may be feeling. The best way to develop this skill is to practice and learn from what works and what doesn't.

What you can do

• Use the goals agreed with your clients as leverage to help them move forward.
• Respect the ways your clients wish to be held accountable.
• Be clear about the different types of interventions.
• Establish ways of monitoring progress that work for each of your clients.
• Believe in your clients, and challenge them to be their best.

16
coaching pitfalls

In this chapter you will learn:
- about common pitfalls that create problems in coaching and how to avoid them
- how the company culture can sometimes be the problem
- what to do when the client is not engaged.

Coaching isn't all plain sailing

As you may already have gathered from various discussions so far in this book, coaching isn't all plain sailing. Sometimes you hit choppy waters, and the boat gets bounced around a lot. Sometimes there's no wind to fill the sales, and you just bob along. And sometimes the crew don't seem to be getting on, and there's talk of a mutiny on board. Coaching looks easy. And to a degree it is easy. But it's not always easy to do it well. There are many potential problems and pitfalls the unwary can fall prey to which can scupper the chances of reaching dry land.

When the coach is the problem

Sometimes it's the coach that causes the problem for a whole host of reasons. Here are some things you should avoid if you want to support your client in making progress. If you skim ahead through the next couple of pages it may seem like quite a long list but the good news is that all these mistakes are 'fixable'. All you have to do is become aware that you're doing them and then decide to do something about them.

Needing to be the 'expert'

A common problem, especially for coaches who come from a consulting or training background, is needing to be an 'expert'. So deeply is this way of behaving ingrained in their psyche that it's hard to shake off. But shake it off you must. Being right, impressing your client and demonstrating how clever you are can be useful in many areas of business – but not when you're coaching. An ego-driven approach is counter-productive. The whole essence of coaching is 'not knowing' – the very opposite of being an expert.

Giving advice and guidance

The biggest challenge for most coaches is to stop giving their clients advice and guidance. In everyday life that's what many of us – especially men – do as a matter of course when someone is stuck or has a problem. But it's really not appropriate in coaching. Your aim is to encourage and empower the person by eliciting their own solution. Not giving advice can be particularly difficult when you have a lot of knowledge about the subject in question or you've coached on it a number of times in the past. If you must share information – and sometimes it does make sense to give your client a 'shortcut' – make it clear you are briefly stepping outside the coaching relationship.

Diagnosing the problem

Once you've cut a few notches on your coaching bedpost it's easy to slip into thinking like an amateur psychologist. Your new client starts talking about what's going on for them, or you sift through their pre-coaching questionnaire, and you 'diagnose' their problem there and then. 'She's got low self-esteem,' you think, or 'he needs to be more efficient with time'. But it's not for you to decide what's 'wrong' with the person. Once you do that you have a point of view that unconsciously directs the kind of questions you ask – and you're no longer working to their agenda.

Needing to fix the client

Having diagnosed their client's problem, some coaches – but mercifully few – feel the need to 'fix' them. This oversteps the mark. No one is 'broken' or 'wrong' – they're just doing the best they can given the experiences and opportunities they've had to date. The coach's role is to support their clients in achieving what they want.

Coaching clients as if they're all the same

Another common mistake is to take a one-size-fits-all off-the-peg approach to coaching, following the same procedure with everyone you see. That just doesn't work. People are unique individuals, and your sessions need to be tailor-made for each one. You may have a number of processes you like to use, and some preferred questions, but they should be adapted to the requirements of a particular client.

Wanting to 'make a difference'

Wanting to be a coach often comes out of a desire to make a difference', to see people develop and grow. That's a noble, worthy aim, but don't allow it to make you try too hard to help your client. They'll feel the pressure of your need for them to 'have a breakthrough' or 'achieve their goals' – and that, paradoxically, will inhibit them for doing so, as well as feeling uncomfortable in the face of your expectations. If you back-off and trust them to do it they'll find their own way.

Not holding them big

How much could your clients achieve? You don't really know. But if you're not careful you could limit them by thinking too small yourself – because to a degree they'll take their cue from you. Maybe they're ready to take a giant step, so it's important to 'hold them big' and believe they have the potential to do whatever they set their mind to.

Requiring accountability

Some coaches get annoyed with their clients when they don't do things they say they will, or won't agree to be accountable for anything in the first place. But not everyone wants to work that way. Some clients don't want to do 'homework' between sessions or commit to carrying through with certain actions, and coaches should respect and accept that preference and not regard it as representing a lack of commitment.

Wanting your client to take on your life beliefs and values

You have your beliefs and values, and your clients have theirs. Often they'll be different. But some coaches can't accept that. They feel they're more 'evolved' or 'developed' than the people they're working with, and expect them – sometimes consciously and sometime unconsciously – to adopt the coach's principles in place of their own.

Dominating the conversation

Some coaches are extrovert, enthusiastic and full of energy – and as a result they end up talking quite a lot. Occasionally this will be appropriate, but most often not. You need to give clients space in which to think, and then to articulate their thoughts – and that won't happen if you're chattering nineteen to the dozen. Unless there's good reason – and sometimes there is – the coach should be speaking for no more that 30 per cent of the session, and ideally less. Don't dominate the conversation. Ask short questions that elicit long answers, and keep any comments brief and to the point.

Using your latest insight

Another common pitfall is when you come across something new. Maybe you've recently read a book on Cognitive Behavioural Therapy and found it really enlightening. And there will be a temptation to introduce some of the ideas into your coaching. There's nothing wrong with this in principle – continuing with your own personal development is essential – but newly acquired knowledge needs to be used appropriately. Take care not to inflict your latest 'ah ha' on an unsuspecting client.

Following your own agenda

It's one thing saying you need to follow your client's thread and let them drive the agenda and quite another actually doing so. Something that often gets in the way is the coach's 'quest' – the thing that's most important to them. It may be to come up with a measurable goal or to become crystal clear about the situation. Both can be useful, but only if they're what the client wants as well.

Getting caught up in the client's 'story'

Your client's life, issues and goals will often be fascinating, and it can sometimes be a bit like watching a soap opera or TV drama unfold week after week. But don't allow yourself to get caught up in their story. A good coach pays more attention to the process than the content of what the client says, noting themes and patterns, and listening at a deeper level than who said what to whom. If you ever get intrigued by what might happen in the 'next episode', it's you that's 'lost the plot'.

Not being prepared to challenge

To be an effective coach for your clients you need to be prepared to challenge them to be their best and achieve their goals – if you don't you'll be failing them. This is particularly important in the executive coaching world, when you'll be judged as much on the business's return on investment as on the development of the individual you're working with. Don't fall into the trap of telling your clients what you think they want to hear. A weak, nice coach is no coach at all.

Not looking after yourself

Dedicated coaches look after their health and well-being. If you work long hours or take too much on, or over-indulge in tobacco, alcohol or drugs, or fail to get enough sleep, you won't have sufficient energy to be there for your clients. So take care of yourself and make sure you're in a good state for your clients.

Sorting out your own issues

Just because you're a coach it doesn't mean you don't have issues of your own to deal with. 'It's almost a cliché in the world of therapy,' says Michael Breen, a Consultant and NLP Trainer, 'most patients are soon cured of their therapists' problems'. The same can happen in coaching. You find your attention irresistibly drawn to the issues your client has that are also issues for you. It's almost as if you're looking in a mirror, and part of you hopes for some vicarious benefit through discussing them. Don't allow this to happen. Sort as much of your 'stuff' out as possible before becoming a coach, and monitor yourself carefully to make sure you don't get hooked when you recognize one of your 'demons' in a client.

Recognizing when you don't have all the answers

Sometimes a deep underlying issue may come to the surface when you're coaching someone. At first you think it's okay and then you realize you've taken something on that you're ill-equipped to deal with – maybe the person has some psychological disorder. Whatever you do don't pretend you can fix anything. It's important to recognize when you're out of your depth and refer the client to someone who has the appropriate skills.

When the client is the problem

Sometimes, though, the problem is less about the coach and more to do with the client. They're just not engaged in the process, they have a misunderstanding about what coaching entails, or they're just not ready to change. All three are barriers to coaching, and need to be addressed by the coach once recognized.

Before you decide that the problem really lies with the client take a long hard look at yourself. In what way might you be contributing to the response you are getting? Double check the previous list and review how you set up the original contract. If this doesn't solve it take a look at the list of items in this section for further clues about what might be going wrong.

The client is looking for advice or therapy

Coaching is a relatively new profession, and many people are confused about what it involves and what it delivers. Some imagine it's the same as therapy or counselling, and expect you just to wave a magic wand and sort their issues out for them.

You can have a similar situation in executive coaching. Clients sometimes get the idea that it's like consulting, and think you're going to go into their company and give them solutions to all the challenges they're facing.

You can avoid these pitfalls by making it abundantly clear on your website, in any brochure and during any discussions you have what exactly is involved in coaching. It will normally become apparent in the first session, occasionally the second, that they expect you to do all the work. If that happens you need to find out what they want. If that's not what you offer, then you have no choice but to 'resign' them, perhaps suggesting somewhere else – a therapist or consultant – where they can go.

When all the client wants is tea and sympathy

Most people who come to coaching genuinely want to change – and are willing to engage in the sometimes challenging and often uncomfortable process of transforming themselves. Occasionally, though, you'll discover they're not really 'up for it'. They're happy to talk about their problems – often at considerable length – but are less inclined to do anything about them.

If you get a sense that all they want is 'tea and sympathy' you have a choice. You can say that's not what you offer, and let them go, or continue to work with them in the hope that the part that does want to change, and which brought them to you in the first place, gets its wishes honoured.

Over a period of time this resistance to change may disappear as they become aware that other possibilities exist for them. But sometimes the person's self-protection system remains firmly in place, so they don't have to face the truth about themself which they may not be ready, or willing, to handle. With the support of their coach they may be able to grow through this and make the change they want.

When the relationship is the problem

Sometime it's not just the coach and not just the client that's creating an issue; it's the relationship between them. Here are three pitfalls that can be avoided with a little care and thought.

You haven't managed the client's expectations

One of the commonest pitfalls in life coaching is not managing the client's expectations. It's all too easy to 'hype' up what you offer on your website and promotional emails – promising a tangible improvement after one session and a complete transformation by the end of the programme – with every goal achieved and the client's life well and truly sorted.

People can take such claims literally and then get disappointed and frustrated when you don't deliver. Of course you want to build your business, and that won't happen if you say you're 'not bad all things considered'. But you need to be realistic, and only promise what you can deliver.

Sometimes prospective clients will ask whether you have expertise and experience in a particular area of interest to them – such as entrepreneurship or career change – and you should always answer honestly. If they think you know more than you actually know, that's a recipe for conflict down the line.

Projection and transference

Anyone working one-to-one with people over a period of time needs to be aware of the issue of transference and projection. It's well known to therapists and others in the 'helping' professions, and generally covered as part of their training. But that's not always the case with coaching.

The essence of this issue is that we all unconsciously 'project' onto others certain qualities in our own nature that we dislike or disown – such as being thoughtless or procrastinating. The things we criticize in others are often the things we like least about ourselves. Putting them 'out there' protects us from having to face them in ourselves.

Transference is where emotions and behaviours, originally experienced in childhood are displaced – they reappear in current relationships. What this means is that after a period of time the client can start to experience the coach as their father or mother, which at its most extreme can lead to issues of dependency and compliance or rebellion and sabotage. The coach also has issues, of course, which leads to counter-transference – where they project certain feelings onto the client.

This is not usually a significant problem in shorter relationships – the typical six-session programme. But when coaching goes on longer, say a dozen sessions or more, it's a good idea to reflect on whether any projection or transference is occurring. If you feel it is, coaching supervision can help in surfacing and sorting any issues that come up.

There's a mismatch between client and coach

Sometimes you don't hit it off with clients. It may not even be something you can put your finger on. The chemistry just isn't right. And it's not working. This doesn't happen that often. You – and they – normally pick up any potential problems of this kind when you first chat. Occasionally, though, you both dismiss it and go ahead. Then it rears its head when you get into the coaching. Don't just assume you can coach anyone. Even with the best of intentions it doesn't always work. Trust your intuition. If you think there are going to be problems for any reason don't proceed.

When the company is the problem

Sometimes there are three parties to the coaching. As well as the client and coach there's also a company – and this can create a number of complications that it's useful to be aware of.

When the client isn't engaged

When people are paying good money to be coached, they normally engage with the process. But if they've been told to participate as part of a company change programme or their boss has said they need coaching to fix a problem, they may not be as keen.

If you're a manager coaching your team you'll be able to pick up the tell-tale signs of suspicion or opposition fairly quickly. If you're an executive coach you may have been briefed ahead of time and are likely to be prepared for it.

Whatever your starting point, look out for signs of resistance such as not coming up with ideas, giving brief answers to questions, or not contributing much and so on. If your intake session was executed thoroughly, however, you're likely to uncover any issues like this straight away.

If you're an external coach resolving the problem may be relatively easy, because you'll be seen as a neutral third party and the confidentiality agreement means people will usually open up and tell you what's on their mind.

When you're an internal coach you have to create the space and climate for your clients to be able to say what they truly feel. Either way once issues like this are out in the open you can usually find a way forward together that has real value to the individual you're coaching as well as meeting any organizational goals. Scepticism will diminish once trust is established.

If they really don't want coaching at all, to some extent it's a waste of their time and yours.

Handling company culture

When you're coaching in-company or acting as an external executive coach you need to take a holistic approach and ask yourself, 'Is it the company culture that's holding them back?'

Sometimes people want to change but don't feel they can because it would conflict with 'the way things are done round here' – and they could be reluctant to question the status quo. While having a common identity and purpose can be useful in an organization it has its downsides too. If a client frequently blames the company system they're giving you a big clue that culture is part of the mix you've got to manage if you're going to help move them forward.

Sample dialogue
Client: There's no point in me suggesting any new ideas – it's just not how this company operates. Every instruction comes down from the top.
Coach: What would happen if you made an exception and gave it a go this time?
Client: It would be a waste of time – guaranteed to hit the bin straight away.

Coach: Who else might be interested in supporting your idea?
Client: The Finance Director should because he'll be keen to save money.
Coach: Great. Who else can you influence?

The 'Wheel of Work' could be used at this stage too because it allows your client to look at the relationships between different aspects of the company (see Chapter 8).

You can revisit the contents of this chapter again and again after each coaching session. It's by no means a definitive list of coaching pitfalls, but it's a useful place to start if your coaching barometer looks like it's falling or becoming too hot to handle.

What you can do

- After every coaching session review what took place and keep an eye out for any coaching pitfalls you may have stepped into.
- Create your own list of things to watch out for when you are coaching – everyone has 'favourites' they tend to default to.
- Discuss your progress with other coaches or a coaching supervisor if you have one.

17

drawing things to a close

In this chapter you will learn:
- how to end the coaching relationship
- how to know when you've finished
- about re-contracting
- what to do if your clients want to continue the relationship indefinitely
- what to do in the final session
- how to consolidate learning
- about change and progress
- how to take the next step
- how to complete with a sponsor or if you are line manager.

The final session

They say that all good things come to an end – and that's certainly true of coaching. It's rare for a relationship to continue indefinitely, for year after year. In fact, the end is often defined at the beginning – you contract for a specific number of sessions, after which you're done.

The final session – often the sixth – is usually a 'completion' session, so the coaching relationship can be brought to a satisfactory conclusion. Running it as a normal coaching session and then just saying goodbye would feel strange for both the coach and the client. Things need to be brought to a proper close, like putting a full stop at the end of a sentence.

There's no 'checklist' you must follow when doing a completion session. What you cover will depend on you and your client. But generally you'll be looking forward and looking back, reflecting on how things were when you started and what the next steps should be. It's also a time for summarizing progress and celebrating successes.

Are you really done?

Of course you may not actually be done. Just because you contracted for a specific number of sessions when you started doesn't necessarily mean that you have to stop. The client may wish to continue, and you should certainly discuss that option with them as you approach the final session. Depending on where they are with their issues, and what remains to be done, they might like to re-contract. This could be for another agreed term – six more sessions or possibly only three. Or you could keep it open ended, taking it just one session at a time if you're close to finishing something off or the client would prefer things to proceed that way.

Cost will obviously be an issue for some clients, and for some sponsoring companies. Their budget may only allow for the number of session originally contracted, and they simply won't be able to afford any more. So you have to bring things to a close even though in reality there's more work to be done. Eventually, though, for whatever reason, you'll find yourself approaching the final session, and will need to ensure things are concluded well.

What if your client wants to continue the relationship indefinitely?

But what if your client or their company can afford to continue, and they would like to do so indefinitely? Well, as long as you both feel there's value in the sessions, and only when you're sure the client isn't becoming dependent on the coach, why not? Some coaches have clients they've worked with for years. One entrepreneur we know regards his coach as a kind of 'personal trainer', who helps keep his personal and professional life in peak condition, and they meet every fortnight.

Some companies offer their senior managers a 'coach for life' for this very reason. But executive and business coaches should be aware that HR professionals often have in mind their need to satisfy two goals – one for the individual and the other for the organization. This means they can be reluctant to support anything that's open-ended because they don't find it easy to measure the benefit to the company. They'll also seek, understandably, to avoid their staff becoming reliant on the coach.

But who says a particular coaching relationship should only run for a finite period? Athletes, football teams and performers don't change their coach every five minutes – they often keep them for a long time. The advantage is that the coach really gets to know them, and a strong bond is established. With a longer relationship the coaching can tend to go deeper and wider because of the understanding between the two parties.

However, this familiarity has its downsides too. The coach can become so used to the client's behaviours, thinking processes and beliefs they fall into the 'trap' of accepting the way they are rather than challenging the status quo. It can all get rather 'cosy', and turn into a pleasant little chat, with the coach adding little if any value.

That's why some business executives like to have a coach all the time but switch coaches periodically to get fresh input and a new perspective on things. The drawback with switching coaches is that each time the client has to go back to the beginning again and explain what they are working on.

Should you ever get to the stage where the client anticipates your questions and starts to answer them before you've asked them it's certainly time for them to move on. The bottom line is that it's the coach's responsibility to recognize if the client's becoming dependent on them and do something about it.

The ultimate aim of any coach should be to do themself out of a job – to become redundant. Clients need to reach the point where they're able to 'fly the nest' and do without the support of the coach. What this means for each person will depend upon their particular issues – but they will generally have greater self-awareness, be more resourceful and be capable of taking ongoing responsibility for progressing their issues independently.

The final session

So you need to leave the client in a position where their improved ability for self-reflection and increased behavioural flexibility means they have many more choices available in dealing with problems when they arise in the future. However, some clients may not be fully ready to 'fly the nest' – their wings may not yet be strong enough. But they have no option because they cannot, or their company will not, finance any further sessions. Your aim then should be to prepare them as best you can for the next stage in their life.

Preparing for the completion session

Having agreed with your client that the next session will be the last, you need to flag up – as you did at the beginning in the intake session – that it will be different and more structured. You should explain that you'll be reviewing the coaching and planning the next steps together. This enables them to prepare mentally for the discussion.

Amanda sometimes suggests to her clients they spend some time making notes on their experiences before the final meeting. This allows more opportunity in the actual session to celebrate achievements and to explore future direction. She recalls one client who sent her an email with 24 individual successes she attributed to coaching over a period of just three months. These ranged from, 'I am procrastinating less and less. I either act or prioritize and work out when I want to do something' to, 'I am more aware of, and have experienced, how being present can enable me to be in a flow state and therefore use even more of my creativity and intuition in my work and in other areas of my life.'

You need to prepare for the session too, perhaps spending a little more time than you would normally. Look back on any notes you may have made on past sessions, and pull the threads together in your mind. How do you feel the coaching went? What have been the successes? What have been the challenges?

Running the completion session

In practice, the final session may not be given over fully to completion. There may be some issues that need to be addressed relating to discussions in the previous meeting. Or they might have experiences they want to talk about before moving into completion. It's up to you as a coach to manage the time: allow sufficient space for them to feel anything outstanding has been handled well while leaving enough for completion so it doesn't feel rushed. This balancing act can sometimes be a tricky one.

Leave the client in a good place

One of the most important things you need to do is to leave your client in a good place, so they're confident in facing the future. You also want them to feel the relationship has been worthwhile – assuming, of course, that it has been. They may have spent a significant amount on the coaching, or their company may have on their behalf. It's essential they believe they've had value for money if you're to get referrals in a life coach setting and a good report/feedback in a corporate situation.

Look back to consolidate learning

You will also want to help them consolidate their learning – to make sure they know consciously what they've learned unconsciously. Some achievements are obvious but many coaches find their clients have grown used to some of the smaller changes they've made. One of the best ways to initiate a discussion is to ask an open question, which you could choose to phrase metaphorically.

Sample dialogue

Coach: As you look back over the last five sessions, what kind of journey would you say you've had?

Client: Well, hmmm, let me think. (Pauses) I don't really know. (Pauses again) I guess I'd probably describe it as a magical mystery tour.

Coach: (Smiles) In what sense?

Client: Well, there have been so many surprises along the way. And I never really knew where I was going. The general direction – yes, of course – but some of the side roads took me places I never expected. And I think I surprised myself too …

Coach: How did you surprise yourself?

Client: In so many ways, actually. I had this view of myself as someone who was not very efficient. A bit of a procrastinator. Always in a muddle.

Coach: And how do you think of yourself now?

Client: (Laughs) I'm sometimes still like that. But not very often. I've stopped putting things off. I just get stuck into them.

Coach: What's changed?

Client: I realized what I was doing to create the inefficiency and muddle, and I did something about it. It's as simple as that.

Coach: It is simple when you look back on it. What else has been magical and mysterious about the last three months?

Client: I suppose I've got to know some parts of my personality a lot better – parts I was only dimly aware of before.

Coach: Such as?

Client: Well I've always lacked confidence when dealing with people at work, and I've sometimes allowed them to trample over my beliefs and values by not being assertive enough. But in our third session I discovered a part of myself that knows how to stand up for itself when an important principle gets violated.

Coach: I remember that was a profound session for you. What's been the effect on your life?

Client: I don't let people get away with any of that any more. If they try, I give them a look that says 'Don't mess with me' and they often back down straightaway.

(Coaching continues)

Once you get started, people normally volunteer thoughts on how they've changed through the coaching relationship. If they get stuck – or can't even begin – it may be worth going back to some of the material you worked with during the Intake session, such as the Pre-coaching Questionnaire, Wheel of Life (or Work) and list of Primary Focus topics. You could ask them to re-do the Wheel and talk about the differences, or see how many – if any – of the primary focus items still apply. Then give your perspective on the coaching relationship. What kind of journey it has been for you, as the coach. Take this opportunity to point out the changes you've observed and celebrate the successes you've seen your client achieve.

Change and progress

What if there's been little change or progress?

Not every coaching relationship delivers dramatic change. Sometimes there's only a little progress. Very occasionally not much at all. What if that's been the case? Do you pretend everything went great, and your client has been utterly and totally transformed? Of course not. That would not only be ridiculous, it would also be unprofessional. You need to 'keep it real' and acknowledge how things have actually been, not how you would like them to have been.

Making it sustainable

Whatever level of change, growth or development has occurred, you want to make sure it's sustainable – that it doesn't fade away like spring flowers once the coaching relationship is over. So in the completion session it's valuable to discuss with your client ways of making sure the learning you've identified lasts well into the future. You may already have done some work in this area during the 'meat' of the coaching sandwich – the sessions in-between the 'bread' of the Intake and Completion sessions. This is the time to tie up as many of the loose threads as you can, so any new behaviours, values, thoughts, beliefs and capabilities feel a natural and normal part of their life in the future. Talking about the various situations your client will find themselves in and how they'll handle them differently – known as 'future-pacing' in NLP – will help ensure the learning kicks in automatically when needed without conscious intervention.

Taking the next step

Something else you need to consider is what's outstanding on your client's 'To Do' list. It's rare, even in a relatively long coaching relationship, for everything that ends up on their Primary Focus sheet to get ticked off. If that ever happens you really are done! What usually transpires is that, once they get into the coaching, clients start to add things they want to tackle they weren't aware of in the beginning. That means you can end up with more goals at the end of six sessions than you had at the outset. So there will almost always be 'unfinished business' – things your client was working on that haven't been completed. How do you deal with this 'work in progress'?

More often than not clients will be going from having you as a coach to having no coach at all – and initially that can be a big step. Having someone to support them in dealing with their issues quickly becomes a habit. When it comes to an end the person will have to rely more on their own resources. Happily, if you've been effective as a coach you'll have assisted the client in developing greater self-reliance and self-confidence, so they're better able to handle situations themselves.

In the completion session, therefore, it makes sense to look at what the person still needs to work on, and how they can do so under their own steam. This can be done in various ways, depending on the client and how they want to develop. Some prefer to discuss things in general terms, with them taking up the reins themselves to drive things forward. Others find it useful to have a more structured, detailed Personal Development Plan. If so, you should take some time out in the completion session to help them formulate one.

Creating a personal development plan

There's no right or wrong way of doing a Personal Development Plan. As long as it works for the person using it that's all that matters. One simple way is to take a sheet of A4 paper and draw a number of columns relating to what they want to do, when they want to have done it by and what resources they might need to help them achieve it.

As always, make sure the goal is positively stated (what you want rather than what you don't want) and the timescale is specific rather than open-ended. With everything else you need to cover in the completion session, you may not have much time to come up with a detailed plan, and your final piece of 'homework' for your client – or the first item on the action

plan, depending on how you think of it – could be to flesh out
the plan itself.

Goal	Timescale	Resources and actions
Be on time more	In three months	Plan better/leave earlier/ assign a buddy to act as 'conscience'
Present confidently	Six months	Practise! Get feedback. Book a place on a course
Increase income by 10%	By end of year	Seek promotion/discuss with boss
Stop interrupting people	One month	Focus on listening better

figure 5 Simple personal development plan

Client becomes coach

You might also suggest your client becomes their own coach.
Having seen you in action over a number of sessions they'll have
some idea of what's involved. There are plenty of 'coach
yourself' books out there to guide them. Keeping a journal will
help them maintain their awareness of themself and others. Or
they may consider going on a personal development course
relevant to the direction in which they're heading.

Remind your clients that ongoing change is about continually
being prepared to take risks and overcoming the fear of doing
something different. As Rhonda Britten says in her book
Fearless Living (2001), 'It's about sticking your neck out. It's
about finding the courage to take risks, to change, and to keep
going even if you falter.'

Keeping in touch

One way to provide support in the early days after the coaching
ends is to call your client or send them an email a few weeks
after the final session to make sure they're okay and everything's
on track. This can also be good from a business perspective – it's
a way of 'hugging' your customers. When they know you care

about them they're more likely to return to you if they need further coaching and to recommend you to friends and colleagues.

Completing with a company sponsor

Executive coaches usually have a final meeting with the sponsor who commissioned and paid for the coaching. Since the content of the coaching sessions is normally confidential – the company only gets 'headlines' – the focus will often be on the effectiveness of the coaching in relation to the reasons it was commissioned in the first place.

Make sure you allow the sponsor time to talk about their perspective of the results – it can be a good idea to let them go first. The changes someone makes during coaching are usually reflected in their day-to-day behaviours and will almost certainly have been picked up by colleagues and bosses. Such feedback is useful in letting the coach and client know how the company thinks the coaching went.

Clients will often want to describe the coaching from their viewpoint when it ends. The aim is to reach the point where everything that needs to be said has been said, and it feels complete.

Completion sessions for managers who coach

Managers who coach may continue to work with a team member for several years or until they switch departments or leave the organization. Although this is a different situation it can still be useful to 'draw a line in the sand' under a particular issue once progress has been made or where a specified goal is achieved.

If not you'll never have a chance to celebrate success, or experience the satisfying feeling of having achieved what you set out to do, before moving on to the next target in a relentless fashion.

What you can do

- Each time you coach someone, keep notes for use in the final session.
- Set aside time to prepare for completion – don't just try to bluff it.
- Keep a log of good ideas to draw on for future completion sessions.

18

developing as a coach

In this chapter you will learn:
- about the importance of practice
- how to assess your coaching skills
- how to continue your professional development as a coach.

Honing your skills

You can't stand still or you'll get left behind. Any coach worth their salt will recognize the importance of developing their skills, knowledge and experience of coaching. This chapter shares some of the secrets of what successful coaches do to keep their skills honed, including:

- asking for feedback
- setting up a coaching circle
- attending courses
- receiving coaching supervision
- reading about coaching and related subjects
- hiring a coach yourself
- learning from other coaches
- working towards a coaching qualification
- getting lots and lots of practice.

The payback will be that you are more effective as a coach and more successful in business.

Practice, practice, practice

While increasing your knowledge and improving your skills are obviously important elements in moving your coaching forward, it's experience that makes all the difference. The more you coach the better you'll get. It's as simple as that. The secret is practice, practice and more practice. The more hours you clock up the more you'll learn what works and what doesn't.

It's all too easy to get out of practice if you don't coach very often and that can lead to a lack of confidence – which is essential for good coaching. Your clients are 'learning to tightrope walk', and need to be assisted by someone who gives them the feeling they won't fall – or if they do they'll be caught. This means you need to be actively coaching. 'You keep the saw sharp by using it', as the saying goes, and even if you're not getting paid initially, you'll want to maintain your coaching skills by regular use.

Assessing your skills as a coach

One of the best ways to evolve your skills is to assess where you are now. Once you know your starting point you can decide on the best way to address any gaps. It's all about giving yourself feedback and challenging your own performance. Effectively it means coaching yourself.

Start by spending some time reflecting on your coaching. Ask yourself: How can my coaching be even better? What am I skilled at? What needs some work? How can I expand my range of questions? Which tools and techniques do I rely on and which don't I use much at all?

You might find you rely on a small number of tried-and-tested questions and techniques – and as a result your coaching has gone a bit stale. Perhaps you realize you don't challenge your clients very much, and tend to be 'soft' with them. Nor do you vary your questions a great deal, falling back on just a few 'favourites'.

The best approach to take is to draw up a list of coaching skills and competencies – you can use the one below as a starting point – and rate your skill level on a scale of 1 to 10 where 1 suggests considerable room for improvement and 10 indicates mastery.

- Establishes and maintains rapport.
- 'Dances in the moment'.
- Holds clients accountable.
- Seeks permission to offer ideas.
- Listens effectively.
- Asks powerful questions.
- Uses intuition.
- Raises the bar.
- Celebrates successes.
- Challenges and stretches.
- Believes in the client's potential.

Tape your coaching sessions

It's all very well assessing your skills in an abstract way but it's often not enough to get a true picture of what you're actually like. You need to get some external, objective evidence too – by listening to yourself or watching yourself in action.

Ask one or more clients if they'll grant you permission to make a tape recording or video of a coaching session. Let them know it will be used for your development only. (It's a good idea to obtain their agreement in writing.) After the session play the tape and note what you do well and what could be improved – once again ranking yourself out of 10.

Getting feedback from your clients

It's fine to assess yourself but it's only your view – and you won't be aware of your 'blind spots'. No matter how rigorous you've tried to be you can't beat asking someone else – and no one is better than a client because they've experienced you first-hand.

Most won't know much if anything about the 'technical side' of coaching – unless, of course, they happen to be a coach or have read a good book on the subject. But they can let you know if what you're doing is working and which things are better than others.

Many established coaches produce a feedback form which they send clients once the sessions they've been commissioned to do are complete. This can provide high quality information because clients who reply have no reason to misrepresent their views.

Doing a coaching swap

Another source of feedback is other coaches. And a great way of getting it is by doing a coaching swap – you coach them and they coach you. If you're learning to coach you should have no difficulty in setting up a reciprocal relationship, while established coaches will often know other working coaches they can team up with.

What you do is coach normally and then periodically – perhaps every three sessions or so – give each other feedback. The advantage of this arrangement is they know a lot more about coaching than your clients, so the feedback will be more detailed and informed.

Having a coach for a client also means you can try different approaches, takes risks and test new ideas safely to see what happens.

In this type of arrangement no money usually changes hands. It's just a great opportunity for both parties to learn. The added bonus to this is that when you're the client you get to work on one of your current life issues or you can use it to accelerate progress on achieving a goal – just like any other coaching client!

Set up or join a coaching circle

If you just pair up with one person, and coach each other, the relationship is likely to get confused. If you can, it's much better to form or join a small group – a coaching circle (see Figure 6).

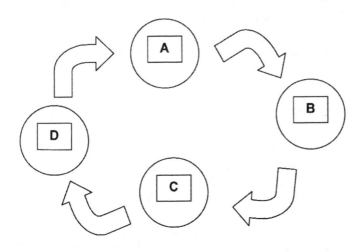

Figure 6 A Coaching Circle: Person 'A' coaches person 'B', 'B' coaches 'C', 'C' coaches 'D' and 'D' coaches 'A'

Most coaches who run these groups arrange the coaching in rounds for a fixed period – say three months – then everyone moves on and gets a new coach and a new client. The circle can go on indefinitely rotating to another person each time. If you keep doing this you'll get feedback from four coaches in a year and have a continuous opportunity to benefit from being coached yourself.

Apart from valuable feedback you'll get to experience a number of different coaches in action which often sparks off ideas for improving what you do.

Improving your coaching skills

Coaching supervision

If you can afford it one of the best ways of improving your coaching skills is to pay for supervision. Well established in counselling, social work and clinical psychology, it's relatively new to the field of coaching. Supervision helps coaches develop and continue with their ongoing professional development and also supports them in handling difficult or complex situations as they arise. Even those who've been coaching for many years recognize the value of working with another equally or more experienced coach on an ongoing basis.

The methods of supervision used in coaching vary from one-to-one training to a mentoring/consultative relationship. Because the concept of supervision arose out of social work and clinical psychology, some of these approaches are now starting to be applied to the field of coaching. One concept came from Kadushin described in his book *Supervision in Social Work* (1976) who describes the functions of supervision as:

- **Educational** – to develop the coach's skills and knowledge.

- **Supportive** – deals with what it feels like to be a coach, and what it feels like to be handling the pressures of the role.

- **Managerial** – works with the coach to establish good policies and practices.

In their book *Supervision in the Helping Professions* (2000), Hawkins and Shohet developed the '7 Eyed Supervision' model which includes:

1 **The client** – time spent on the client's situation, how they handle issues, the decisions they make, their goal, etc.

2 **Coaching interventions** – how the coach is working with the client and considering other possible interventions they could make.

3 **The coaching relationship** – this examines the dynamic between coach and client and explores both conscious and unconscious aspects of the relationship.

4 **The coach** – this encourages the coach to become more self-aware by drawing on their experience or intuitions about what may be going on in the client's internal world.

5 **The parallel process** – this allows the coach to recognize how the dynamics of the client relationship are also playing out within the supervisory relationship.

6 **The supervisor's self-reflection** – where the supervisor shares their perspectives and understanding of the coaching relationship.

7 **The wider context** – this provides the opportunity to discuss ethical, cultural or organizational aspects of the coaching relationship.

Whatever model is used, if any at all, supervision sessions are carried out in either one-on-one/group face-to-face meetings or telephone/email-based sessions. Some supervisors ask their coaches to tape a meeting with a client (having gained their permission in writing).

The tape can then be played with both the coach and the supervisor listening. Then the supervisor gives the coach feedback. The coach can shape their feedback by asking the supervisor to focus on specific aspects they want to improve – but it's probably better to allow the supervisor to point out what they consider to be most important.

If you want to be accredited as a certified coach some organizations such as The International Coaching Federation (ICF) insist on supervision as part of the process. If you're going for this you need to ask your supervisor to give you an overall score. For more details on this take a look at the ICF website – details can also be found in 'Taking it further' on page 226.

Choosing a supervisor

A good place to start if you want to find a coaching supervisor is to approach one of the professional bodies such as the Association for Coaching, The International Coaching Federation or the European Mentoring and Coaching Council. Make sure your supervisor has the right level of know-how to meet your needs. Ideally they'll be an established coach who also has experience in supervision. You may want to check out your supervisor's qualifications and – most importantly – whether their style and approach to coaching fits with yours.

Get a coach yourself

Another great way to grow your coaching ability is to get a coach yourself. There's nothing quite like learning what happens when you're on the receiving end. You'll soon know what works and what doesn't.

If you choose someone who's been coaching for a number of years, they'll have lots of experience, and will probably have developed a wide repertoire of questions to suit different situations. In fact if over a period of time you employ a variety of different coaches it can help you develop flexibility in your approach and significantly improve the results your clients get from your own coaching.

It's all too easy to get into a rut and do the same old thing each time with every client – and that just doesn't work. Coaching needs to be adapted to the needs of the individual. This means you need to be able to be strong and vigorous as well as quiet and silent, driving and challenging as well as supportive and understanding.

Switch coaches

When you choose someone as your coach you may choose to stick with them the next time round because the relationship worked well and feels familiar.

> Amanda has a coach who's a good fit for her – and who she goes back to from time to time. They have shared values and a mutual interest in spiritual growth. She finds her coach immensely practical and has progressed with many of her personal and business goals much more quickly as a result of working with her. One of the added bonuses of having a coach for Amanda is that she experiences first hand a different but complementary style to her own and then goes on to use some of the things she's experienced in her own coaching.

> Steve prefers to switch to a different coach every few months. He knows it's all too easy to choose someone as his coach at a subconscious level who will allow him to avoid his blind spots – and he doesn't want to be let off the hook.

Learning from other coaches

You can learn a lot about coaching by studying excellence in other coaches. It's possible to work out how anyone does pretty much anything by paying close attention to the patterns in their behaviour. If you get the opportunity to observe experienced coaches in action you'll pick up lots of useful tips.

> When Amanda first wanted to build her skills as a coach, she went to seminars delivered by some well known coaches. She not only learnt what they did, she also found out what was important to them – the values and beliefs that drove their behaviour.

Activity

If you have the chance, talk to people whom you know to be good coaches. Ask them questions to find out how they experience coaching.

- What's important to you when you're coaching?
- What are your beliefs about coaching?
- What's the difference that makes the difference in your coaching?
- How do you feel inside when you're coaching?
- What was the most challenging situation you have faced so far? How did you handle it?

Continuing your development

Read personal development books

One obvious but effective way of developing your understanding of people and what makes them tick is to become a personal development book junkie.

With hundreds of titles swelling the shelves you're spoilt for choice. If you often coach people about personal relationships you may find some of John Gray's *Men are from Mars* (2002) books useful. Or, for more general inspiration, pick up some 'be your own life coach' books – where you'll find plenty of ideas to stimulate your own coaching.

Go on a course

Another way you can extend your skills is to complete a relevant course of study. How about an Open University degree in Psychology? Or an MSc in Coaching? Suggested courses can be found in 'Taking it further' on page 219.

If spending years studying isn't your bag you could sign up for some shorter courses on topics such as, Neuro-Linguistic Programming or Cognitive Behavioural Therapy. Subjects like these expand your range of knowledge and add further tools to your coaching kit bag.

There are also various forums on the internet where you can join a mailing list or participate in a chat room on a range of related topics. You can post questions and get feedback or comments from other members. Some forums are dedicated purely to coaching; others are more general in nature.

Improve business knowledge

If you're an executive or business coach you'll need to keep up to speed with what's happening in the corporate sector so you can talk knowledgeably to your clients. That means reading magazines such as the *Economist*, a broadsheet newspaper, and the latest business titles on subjects such as change management, leadership and marketing – as well as classic titles such as *The Fifth Discipline* (1990) by P M Senge.

Want to break into the business market but don't have a corporate background and need to establish your credibility? One way might be to do an MBA, which is held in high regard by many business people.

And since it's always useful to add another string to your bow, you might consider becoming licensed to use a profiling tool such as Extended DISC, MBTI or Firo B. Although they are mostly employed in a business setting they can also provide some useful insights for life coaching clients prepared to meet the cost of having a profile done.

Work towards coaching accreditation

Another excellent way of advancing your coaching is working towards accreditation at a recognized association or federation. This can require attendance at specified courses, putting in a certain number of paid-for coaching hours, and receiving a number of hours of coaching supervision.

Develop authenticity as a coach

One important aspect of how you develop your coaching style relates to the way in which coaching fits with your own sense of identity and, if you feel you have one, purpose in life. How does this affect the experience others have when being coached by you?

Our experience from attending and running courses on coaching is that once people connect to what's really important to them their coaching really starts to come alive. They're no longer using processes or techniques, but communicating with their clients at a much deeper level.

Most coaches we know love learning and get a buzz out of discovering new things that add to their coaching tool-kit.

> Steve has a playful, slightly provocative side which, when he first
> started coaching, he kept well under wraps, thinking it
> inappropriate to use. However, as he felt more comfortable being
> himself when coaching, he found that his natural, challenging
> style was effective in some situations and, from the feedback he
> received, perceived as a lot more 'real'.

Perhaps most of all they have a thirst for making what they do
more and more effective. They take a pride in their profession
and want to continue to ensure they offer their very best to their
clients.

What you can do

- Join or set up your own coaching circle and start practising.
- Design a feedback form you can send to your clients.
- Find yourself a supervisor with the right skills to help you
  develop as a coach.
- Create a log of useful ideas for improving your coaching.

19

business aspects

In this chapter you will learn:
- how to set up as a sole trader, partnership or limited company
- how to keep business accounting records
- about marketing your business, building client relationships and selling your services
- how to track your performance and test your marketing strategy
- what's involved in winning work from organizations.

Creating a coaching business

The driving force behind many independent coaches is a desire to make a difference to people's lives. Focusing on what's required to make a success of their business is not always uppermost in their minds. But if you want to earn a living from coaching you have to know how to set up and run a thriving practice. There's more to it than meets the eye and coaches don't always have the experience and skills to sell their services or manage accounts.

One of the most important things to be aware of is that you need to work on your business not just in it. This means dividing your time between coaching, winning new clients and managing the operational side. It can be quite a juggling act.

Self-employment can sometimes mean a drop in living standards – at least in the short term. You need money to cover holidays and don't get paid when you're sick. But if you've done your sums right it can be worthwhile. Sixty-three per cent of new business owners say that running a business is stressful but 90 per cent don't regret doing it.

The purpose of this chapter is to get you pondering over some of the key things you need to consider about running a successful business, such as:

- setting up an office at home
- putting money aside for tax
- whether or not to charge VAT
- opening a bank account
- creating a marketing strategy
- maintaining client relationships
- writing proposals and pitching for work.

Choosing a business name

Many people agonize over what to call their company. One option is to trade under your name with 'coaching' added – Amanda Vickers Coaching. Or you could go for something completely different, such as Infinite Potential. Names matter. They affect the entire way in which your company is viewed. So spend some time getting yours right. Using your own name can work in the life coaching market, because it makes you sound personable and approachable. But it can also say to the world that you're a 'one-man-band'. There's nothing wrong with that unless you're an executive coach pitching after a big piece of work with a lot of other coaches – and you don't sound right or look big enough. Whatever name you choose make sure it's not already in use by a competitor. Check on the internet to see if the domain name's available, and find out whether it's been registered at Companies House (see 'Taking it further').

Sole trader, partnership or limited company

One of the first things you need to decide is what kind of company structure you want – sole trader, partnership or limited company. Ideally you'll want to talk it over with an accountant, bank manager, or solicitor – they are the first three people you should appoint if you don't already have such advisers. Whenever possible choose them on the basis of a personal recommendation. Below are the main advantages and disadvantages of each type of company structure.

Sole trader

There's nothing simpler than setting up a business as a sole trader. There's no 'red tape' at all. You can just begin. The advantage is that you really are your own boss with no one else to answer to. All you need to do is inform your local tax inspector that either you've gone from being an employee to being self-employed or are now earning freelance income alongside PAYE (pay as you earn).

Partnership

Most life coaches go the sole trader route because it offers maximum freedom. But if you really don't like working alone, consider a partnership – either with a like-minded colleague who coaches or someone with a business or sales background who could undertake a different role within the company. One of the advantages of going into business with other people is they can contribute skills or experience you don't have. But one problem that can come up is where one partner puts in more time, effort and energy than the other. This can lead to bad feeling and conflict which takes everyone's focus off making the business work. However well you know your partner(s) it's important to get a proper agreement drawn up by a solicitor that covers how you will divide the profits, what happens if one of you dies or wants to leave the company.

Limited company

Very few life coaches or executive coaches go to the trouble of setting up a limited company at the outset. If you're simply aiming to replace your salary with an income from coaching it's not the best option. But if you want to build a big company, going limited makes sense, as the shareholders are not liable as individuals for debts if the company goes bankrupt. That's not particularly likely with coaching, since there's no stock – all that's sold is time. But it can be a sensible precaution if several people are involved.

You can set up a limited company on your own but the easiest was is to get your accountant or solicitor to buy one 'off the-shelf' and then change the name to whatever you want. The cost of forming a company is around £250. Full details on how to form a limited company in the UK are available from Companies House (see 'Taking it further').

Accounting matters

What's most important when you're running your own business is to keep adequate financial records. The simplest system is to use a cash book, from which your accountant produces the finished accounts. If you prefer to use a computer there are a number of financial packages around such as Quickbooks, Cashflow Manager or Sage.

By law you're required to keep all receipts, invoices, expense sheets etc. for at least five years.

If you're trading under your own name it's not essential to have a separate bank account, but it's a lot easier if you do. It doesn't cost that much for a business account if your level of transactions is low, and many banks will give you a year free of charges when you start up.

There are lots of expenses you can legitimately claim which will reduce your tax bill. In the UK under Schedule D (the tax system for self-employed people) you can claim an allowance for services such as gas, electricity and water, some of your telephone bill, postage, stationery and anything that is 'wholly and necessarily' required for coaching. Your accountant will advise you on this if you're unsure about what to claim. His (or her) fee, by the way, is also tax-deductible and worth every penny.

If you're planning to go full-time it's a good idea to prepare a business plan. Most of the banks can provide you with advice or even a CD which includes the format you need to follow. While not essential it does encourage you to project earnings and take account of all outgoings which helps you to assess how much you can expect to earn. It's also a good idea to keep a close eye on cash flow, because lack of it can easily cripple a fledgling business. All you need is a simple spreadsheet showing dates and the amounts of expected outgoings and anticipated sales income. Make sure also that you put money aside for tax. Bills come in twice a year and if you've been successful they can be sizeable.

VAT registration or not?

In the UK if you expect your turnover to be more than £60,000 per annum you need to register for Value Added Tax (VAT). Few life coaches get anywhere near that figure but some executive coaches might. You can, if you wish, register voluntarily if your turnover is below that level. There's no real advantage for life coaches in doing so, but since executive coaches deal with companies it can make them appear more substantial and is worth considering.

If you are working from home

Your accountant will advise you of any issues you need to consider if you plan to work from home. You may, for instance, need to let your mortgage and insurance companies know about the change of use.

It's a good idea to take out Professional Indemnity Insurance in case a client makes a claim as a result of your coaching work. This doesn't happen often, but there are a number of brokers around who specialize in this type of policy. Cover is typically for £1–2m. If people are coming to your premises for coaching it's also wise to take out Public Liability insurance to cover you in the event that someone has an accident or other mishap during their visit.

As well as somewhere to carry out the coaching you'll also need office space – it could be the same room if you have one big enough. There needs to be space for a desk, chair, filing cabinet, computer, printer, phone, answer machine etc.

Establishing a professional image

Your future clients need to feel reassured that they're in safe hands, and that means you have to come across as credible and professional in everything you do.

- **Have your stationery designed and printed professionally** – people can tell if you've knocked something together yourself. It's an investment not a cost.
- **Put the essentials in place** – load your computer with office software packages so your communication and background procedures operate smoothly.
- **Get your own domain name** – it doesn't cost much. Emails that go out from a free account such as Hotmail or Yahoo, or from a BT or Virgin account, give your business an amateur appearance.
- **Create a website** – as soon as you can. This gives the impression that you're established and here to stay.
- **Print brochures and flyers** – these need to look the part too. Make sure yours suit your target audience. Lots of white space makes them look more upmarket.
- **Set up a system for taking messages** – when you're not around or are busy coaching, at the bare minimum you need a dedicated line with an answer phone or virtual assistant.

Personal issues to consider

When you switch to self-employment there are some personal issues you need to take into account:

Pension

If you have a company pension scheme, you'll need to make provisions for continuing with this through a private scheme.

Permanent health and critical illness insurance

You can't afford to be ill when you work for yourself, so consider taking out Permanent Health Insurance (PHI) to compensate you for lost earnings if you're unwell. However, it's not cheap and you need to read the small print carefully because it may not pay out straight away if at all for certain conditions. It can be worth considering taking out critical illness insurance which provides you with a lump sum in the event that you become very seriously ill.

Leasing or buying a car

Quite a few people have company cars and will either need to buy one or lease a car through their business. If you haven't got enough cash at hand to buy a car you may want to lease one. There can be tax advantages of doing so.

Marketing essentials

You need to let prospective clients know that you exist and what you do. That means marketing yourself. The first, crucial step is to identify your target market. Who are your customers? If you're an executive coach you may be aiming at a particular business sector such as retail, finance, or pharmaceuticals. If you're a life coach you may be prepared to take on anyone or prefer to focus on specific issues such as family relationships.

Define your potential clients in as much detail as possible. Get to know everything you can about them. Life coaches should focus on the type of person they aim to attract: the typical age group, marital status, economic position etc. Executive coaches need to find out about the geographical location of their target companies, the number of employees, their attitude to outsourcing and so on.

Once you've defined your target you need to work out what you have to offer them. When there's so much competition around it's important to stand out from the crowd. What makes you different from the rest? What benefits do you offer your clients?

Selling benefits rather than features

Make a list of all the features you plan to offer. Now put yourself in the position of a prospective client. What would be important to you? Challenge each of your answers by asking, 'So what?' And turn each feature into a benefit. People buy services for three main reasons:

1 to satisfy a need.
2 To solve a problem.
3 To feel good.

You need to work out what's in it for the client.

Selling on features
Specialist wealth coach: 'I've worked for 20 years as a financial adviser'.

Selling on benefits
Specialist wealth coach: 'My background in the financial sector means I have lots of experience to offer people who want to manage their money more effectively.'

Selling on features
Executive coaching company: 'All our coaches have psychology degrees.'

Selling on benefits
Executive coaching company: 'Because all our coaches have psychology degrees they're qualified to assist people in understanding how to feel good about life and motivate themselves to achieve their goals.'

Ways of promoting yourself
There are many different ways of promoting yourself, and we've listed a selection that is suitable for someone who's just starting out in the industry.

Public Relations (PR)
One of the best ways to let people know what you do is through PR. If you're a life coach contact your local radio station and volunteer to talk about coaching or send out a press release letting your local newspapers know what you do. Executive coaches can approach trade magazines relating to the industry sector they're targeting. The great thing about PR is it's free – apart from the cost of a stamp or a phone call – and the value you get is far greater than advertising. A 100-word mention in a magazine is worth a full page of advertising because people give more credence to a published article than an advert. Once you build relationships with newspaper and magazine editors you can offer to provide articles or even volunteer to write a regular column.

Advertising

Advertising needs to be continued over a sustained period if it's to bear much fruit – and it doesn't come cheap. If you're a life coach you could consider placing an advert in *Yellow Pages* but there are probably more effective ways to get business such as networking. Whatever happens, don't be tempted to take an advert in your local newspaper or county magazine, because experience shows that the level of response is unlikely to cover the cost.

Cold or warm calling

Executive coaches are likely to spend some time 'cold calling' potential clients. You can get numbers by going through the local telephone directory, *Yellow Pages* or via the internet. It's not an approach that's usually appropriate for life coaches except in the early days when you're making follow-up warm calls to an introductory letter you've sent out. If you want to know more about cold calling read Stephan Schiffman's book *Cold Calling Techniques That Really Work* (2003).

And when you meet someone who expresses an interest in coaching, make sure you follow the lead up with a call or email.

Giving talks

Both life and executive coaches can benefit from offering to give free talks about coaching to local groups such as the Chamber of Commerce, Women's Institute and Rotary Club. Many actively look for speakers, so you'll be pushing at an open door. The local library is also a good source of possible groups you can approach.

Promotional gifts

One good way to attract business is to produce and distribute a free CD/DVD on which you demonstrate your coaching. These days it's relatively inexpensive and can have lots of impact.

Internet marketing

One 'must-have' these days is a website. If you're IT 'savvy' you can create your own; if not you'll need to hire a company to design and host the site. You need to make sure it's found when people do a search, so it's important to get your Search Engine Optimization right (a good website expert will be able to tell you how to get the best results from your site).

It's also important to make it 'sticky' – so people keep coming back – by updating the content frequently and including free articles. You can also send out a quarterly email newsletter with information about personal development in general. Make sure you include an 'opt out' clause when you're sending them to businesses – otherwise it will be treated as spam. If you want to send a newsletter to private individuals you need to obtain their permission first.

And whenever you're sending emails always add a promotional message after your electronic signature – which might just be your contact details – domain name, logo, address, and telephone number. Make it easy for people to get in touch.

Brochures or leaflets
Some coaches direct all requests for information to their website – and don't produce a written brochure, which in the past might have cost a lot of money. However, there are many places you can place a leaflet that exposes you to lots of different clients, such as a doctor's surgery or your local reference library. You should also put a business card or brochure in everything you send out and leave them wherever you go – airports, the gym, hotels, restaurants etc.

Networking
You need to be mixing with your target audience, so attend networking events which they also go to. Coaching is such a personal thing that people often feel more comfortable hiring someone they've met and got to know. Most established coaches – both life and executive – say networking is one of their biggest sources of work. There are a number of organizations who hold networking events or breakfast meetings such as E-cademy and Business Link. To make the most of networking you need to develop an 'elevator pitch', explaining what you do in a short space of time – as if you were travelling from the ground floor to the penthouse in a lift. It's useful to come up with half a dozen specific ways you could help clients so you can match what you say to what people want.

Coaching referral sites
You can add your details to websites that provide a referral service such as The International Coaching Federation or 24/7 Coaching. In some cases you have to become a member first and in others you pay a one off fee.

Testimonials and referrals
The surest way of growing your coaching business is through referrals. When clients tell their friends and acquaintances how

good you are you're bound to get more work. So encourage them to do so. If you're a life coach you might even go so far as to give them money-off vouchers for the first session.

You should also collect as many testimonials as you can because they convince prospects to give coaching a go – and can be featured in your promotional material.

Creating lasting client relationships

Although clients tend to come and go – especially in life coaching – it's important to look after your relationships if you want repeat work and lots of referrals. If they have a good experience they'll come back to you when they next want coaching. It costs twice as much to get a new client as it does to maintain an existing one.

It's the little things that often make the most difference. Do you plan to give your clients a drink when they arrive? Find out their favourite drink and have it ready without having to ask what they want or pass on an article that you think will interest them. It's all about thinking ahead and doing things that are personal for each client.

Jack Mitchell's book on this subject – *Hug Your Customers* (2003) – is well worth a read and much of the content can be applied to any company. He describes it as a mindset and recommends that you don't cut back on things the customer will notice. Because coaching is a people business you have to walk the talk in everything you do.

Record your activity

Set up a database to record every communication you have with a potential or existing client. Establish daily targets and track your progress against the goals you set yourself. Reward your successes even if it's just treating yourself to a massage when you meet your monthly target. See the Sales Action Sheet in the Appendix for an idea of what you can do.

Keep on marketing

You need a constant stream of marketing activity if you're to be successful as a coach. You can't just do it in spurts. And if you get to the stage where you 'need' to do some marketing, because no work – or money – is coming in, you've already left it too late. To avoid feast and famine you have to get a balance between winning the work and doing the coaching. And don't get into a rut, doing the same old thing over and over again.

Vary your marketing mix. Concentrate on PR for a while then do a mail shot. Update the website then do a few talks.

Test marketing

Whenever you introduce a new form of marketing communication test it first to find out how effective it is. This can save you a lot of time, money and effort. If you're an executive coach and have a mail shot you want to send out to 1000 people try it with 100 first.

Establish criteria for success such as 'X' number of people call to enquire or 'Y' sales are achieved after follow up calls. If it works you know you're onto a winner – and can mail the lot. If it doesn't, you can change the content and try again, or trial a completely different method of communicating like an E-Newsletter. Track the performance of all your marketing efforts. If you don't how will you know if they're effective?

Winning business from organizations

If you're an independent executive coach working alone, you'll sometimes be asked to send a potential client an outline of your approach, a brief biography and fee details. For larger pieces of work – especially where there's more than one coach involved – you may need to send a detailed proposal. One of the advantages of networking with other coaches is that you can quickly get together a team when required.

Ingredients of a good proposal

There are many different ways of structuring a proposal. We're suggesting one way that's worked well for us but make sure you match what you do with what your client has asked for. If they want only a one-page overview with fees give them that and no more. Here's a suggested structure:

- **Background/Introduction** – this is your description of the situation the client faces.
- **Our approach to coaching** – explain how you work and the benefits you offer. It needs to give the client a sense of what it's like to work with you.
- **Coach biographies** – include a brief biography of the coaches the client can choose from.

- **Fees** – outline all the costs involved. Don't forget to mention there will be VAT (if you're registered) and travel expenses.
- **Testimonials** – gather a collection of positive comments from satisfied clients and include them in your proposal.

Pitching for business

For some larger pieces of work, you and your team may be required to attend meetings to pitch for the business against other coaching firms.

Seven secrets of successful coaching pitches

1 **Choose the team carefully.** Often with pitches there will be a team present – the business owner and one or more of the coaches who will carry out the work. Identify the strengths and weaknesses of each person and decide who will say what. Everyone needs to speak, and one person needs to be nominated to lead the proceedings.

2 **Consider your client's viewpoint.** What's the client's previous experience of coaching? What are they concerned about? What do they expect?

3 **Prepare well.** What problem does your client want to solve? List the ways the coaching that you offer will solve it. Select the ones you think will appeal most.

4 **Design the structure.** Think about the sequence of the presentation. Say why you are different from the competition. Make abstract ideas tangible.

5 **Keep visual aids to a minimum.** If you must use visual aids, make sure they're relevant and don't contain too many words.

6 **Prepare for questions.** Come up with at least half a dozen tough questions you might face, and work out how you'll answer them.

7 **Practise.** Rehearsing what you plan to say out loud makes a big difference to your confidence. Decide how to handle links between each person speaking.

Get the money in the bank

The sales cycle is not complete until the money is in the bank. This tends to be straightforward for life coaches who are usually paid at the end of each session, or in advance by direct debit if they have a monthly fee arrangement with clients.

If you're an executive coach it's not always that simple. Even if you send out your sales invoices promptly you can find them unpaid a couple of months later. So include a 'payment due by' date and get on the phone as soon as it's overdue. But don't chase the person who commissioned you – contact the accounts department and try to build a relationship with one person in particular. That can oil the wheels. If, after repeated calls – say three or four – you're not getting anywhere, send a formal letter. If that doesn't work, pursue your payment through the small claims court.

What you can do

- Seek ideas and advice from other business owners.
- Create a marketing plan to document your ideas.
- Measure your success and celebrate every milestone.

20

training courses

In this chapter you will learn:
• how to select a training course to meet your needs.

Coaching training companies

You can only learn so much about coaching from a book. Ultimately, if you're serious about the subject, you'll want – or, arguably, need – to go on a course, to get practical experience. But how, when there are so many different courses from such a variety of training providers, do you decide which to go for? The answer to this question depends to a large degree on personal choice and individual learning preferences. Even so, there are also some important issues to consider before you part with your hard earned cash.

Does the company have an established track record?

Choosing a company with an established track record will give you confidence. They must have a reasonably good course or they wouldn't still be in business Of course, every course was brand new at one time and there's something to be said for embracing new ideas and approaches.

How many people does the company have on each course?

Some people learn best in small intimate groups where they get plenty of individual feedback and attention. Others enjoy the variety and stimulation of a large group environment. Coaching training courses can vary in size from 6 to 100 plus. One advantage of a big class is that you get to coach and be coached by a wider range of people.

Is there plenty of opportunity for face-to-face practice and for obtaining feedback?

We strongly recommend you choose a course with a face-to-face element. This is the most effective way of learning to coach through experience. Feedback is invaluable because it allows you to grow your skills at a much faster rate.

Does the company offer teleclasses?

Some coaching training companies include a mixture of distance learning and teleclasses (coaching training with a group that takes place through a telephone conference). This style of learning isn't for everyone but offers flexibility if you have lots of other demands on your time or are geographically remote.

What back-up support does the company provide?

Some companies offer a range of free resources on their website and via newsletters. It's also good to know they have administrative support to sort out any queries you may have.

Does the course provide an opportunity for you to work towards accreditation?

If accreditation is important to you select a course that has been approved by the organization you want to align yourself with.

Does the programme include NLP?

While NLP is certainly not a requirement for coaching it can add an extra edge and level of insight to your work. Some courses provide an introduction as part of the training others insist you attend NLP training beforehand.

How much does the course cost?

Value for money is always an important consideration, especially when practice is so vital. While quantity is by no means better than quality it's worth comparing what various companies offer.

Does the course do 'what it says on the tin'?

If you want to be a life coach you don't want most of the material to be based on the world of business. Conversely, if you want to be an executive coach you want to be sure what you're learning is relevant to the needs of your future clients.

What you can do

- Select a course to attend that suits your learning style and budget to take your skills to the next level.

taking it further

This book is filled to the brim with information that will help you to become an effective coach. But there's always more to discover. This section provides a rich array of resources that will enable you to continue your journey. It includes details of coaching organizations, forums, websites, books, newsletters and tools.

Coaching training companies

Here is a list of websites for some of the companies offering coaching training:

Association for Coaching
www.associationforcoaching.com/

Centre for Coaching
www.centreforcoaching.com/training/

Coaching Development
www.coachingdevelopment.com

Coaching and mentoring
www.coachingandmentoring.com

Coach University
www.coachu.com

CoachVille
www.coachville.com

Comprehensive Coaching U
www.comprehensivecoachingu.com

International Teaching Seminars
www.itsnlp.com

Newcastle College
www.ncl-coll.ac.uk

Newfield Network
www.newfieldnetwork.com

Noble Manhattan
www.noble-manhattan.com

The Oxford School of Coaching and Mentoring
www.oscm.co.uk

The Coaching Academy
www.the-coaching-academy.com

The Coaches Training Institute
www.thecoaches.com

The Performance Solution
www.theperformancesolution.com

The Work Foundation
www.theworkfoundation.com

The UK College of Life Coaching
www.ukclc.net

Various courses are also listed at the Global Coaching Calendar
at www.globalcoachingcalendar.com/

CDs

A useful way of learning about coaching is *The Virtual Coach* CD-Rom available from Speak First – www.speakfirst.com. This training package is designed to promote the value of coaching and develop the skills of people who have already had some coaching training. It's a great refresher and a good way of keeping your skills sharp.

Coaching Skills for NLPers is an audio programme available on a collection of six CDs from The Performance Partnership – www.performancepartnership.com

Shelle Rose Charvet, who is well known for her work on language and metaprogrammes, has produced a set of CDs on Conversational Coaching with the LAB (Language and Behaviour) profile. They're recordings of seminars which focus on using coaching informally in every day situations. For more information go to: www.successstrategies.com

Organizations

Various organizations have evolved to provide support, advice and guidance on coaching. We've listed some of them and suggest you take a look at their websites to get a fuller understanding of their purpose. Many set standards for coaching, inform coaches and clients about coaching and some offer an online coaching referral service.

International Coaching Federation
www.coachingfederation.org

European Coaching Institute
www.europeancoachinginstitute.org

European Mentoring and Coaching Council
www.emccouncil.org

Association for Coaching
www.associationforcoaching.com

International Association of Coaches
www.internationalassociationofcoaches.org

Coaching Foundation Ltd
www.angusmcleod.com

Guild of Master Coaches
www.guildofmastercoaches.com

There are also organizations that can assist you with business issues:

Business Link gives professional business advice, networking opportunities and a helpful e-newsletter.
www.businesslink.gov.uk

Start Out in Business provides plenty of useful online information about starting a business.
www.startoutinbusiness.com

The Institute of Directors is an organization for people in businesses of all sizes. You need to become a member to benefit from most of their services, which include, use of their premises for client meetings, research facilities, courses and networking events.
www.iod.com

Companies House provides information about forming a limited company.
www.companieshouse.org.uk

Coaching Internet forums

There are a number of internet-based coaching forums available. The nature of the business means that coaches can feel isolated. Forums provide a great way of networking from your computer and keeping up to date with current thinking in the coaching industry. Many coaches use this vehicle for expressing their views and shaping the future of coaching. Others use forums as a source of advice on situations they are not sure how to handle.

Coen de Groot (Bristol, UK)
www.eurocoachlist.com

Coach Universe
www.coachuniverse.com

Coaching Academy
www.coachlists.com

The Coaching Foundation
subscribe-coachingfoundation@yahoogroups.com

Life Coach Forum
www.lifecoachwebsolutions.com/coachingforum/index.php

Networking opportunities

There are a number of established organizations geared to helping small businesses network and build their businesses, including:

Ecademy
www.ecademy.com and www.bre.ecademy.com

Business Link
www.businesslink.gov.uk

Chamber of Commerce
www.chamberonline.co.uk

Directories

There are various directories where, for a fee or a membership benefit, you can be listed on a searchable database. These include:

www.247coaching.com

www.coachfederation.org

Books

Here are a few books that will be useful to you as you expand your knowledge and understanding of coaching.

Bavister, Steve and Vickers, Amanda (2003) *Coach – Be Your Best and Beyond*, Hodder & Stoughton.

Britten, Rhonda (2001) *Fearless Living*, Hodder & Stoughton.

Downey, Myles (2001) *Effective Coaching*, Texere Publishing.

Egan, Gerard (1998) *The Skilled Helper*, Brooks/Cole Publishing.

Essex, Arielle (2004) *Compassionate Coaching*, Random House.

Flaherty, James (1999) *Coaching – Evoking Excellence in Others*, Butterworth Heinemann.

Forster, Mark (2000) *Get Everything Done and Still Have Time to Play*, Hodder & Stoughton.

Gallwey, Timothy (2000) *The Inner Game of Work*, Orion Business Books.

Gee, Arianna and Gregory, Mary (2005) *Be Your Own Love Coach*, New Holland.

Harrold, Fiona (2000) *Be Your Own Life Coach*, Hodder & Stoughton.

Landsberg, Max (1996) *The Tao of Coaching*, HarperCollins.

McLeod, Angus, Ph.D. (2003) *Performance Coaching*, Crown House Publishing.

Neenan, Michael and Dryden, Windy (2002) *Life Coaching: A Cognitive-Behavioural Approach*, Routledge.

O'Connor, Joseph and Lages, Andrea (2004) *Coaching With NLP*, Harper Collins.

Peterson, David B., Ph.D. and Hicks, Mary Dee, Ph.D. (1956) *Leader As Coach*, Personnel Decisions International.

Starr, Julie (2003) *The Coaching Manual*, Pearson Education Limited.

Whitmore, Sir John (1999) *Coaching for Performance*, Nicholas Brearley Publishing.

Whitworth, Laura, Kimsey-House, Henry and Sandhal, Phil (1998) *Co-Active Coaching: New Skills for Coaching People Toward Success in Work and Life*, Davies-Black Publishing.

Zeus, Perry and Skiffington, Suzanne (2001) *The Complete Guide to Coaching at Work*, McGraw Hill.

Books to help you establish and grow your business:

Adair, John (2002) *Effective Team building; How to Make a Winning Team*, Pan.

Ashton, Robert (2004) *The Entrepreneur's Book of Checklists*, Pearson Prentice Hall.

Belbin, R. Meredith (2003) *Management Teams: Why They Succeed or Fail*, Butterworth Heinemann.

Covey, Stephen R. (1992) *Principle-Centred Leadership*, Simon & Schuster.

Franks, Lynne (2000) *The Seed Handbook*, HarperCollins.

Gerber, Michael, E (1994) *The E-Myth Revisited*, HarperCollins.

Kouzes, Jim and Posner, Barry (2003) *The Leadership Challenge*, Jossey Bass Wiley.

Reuvid, Jonathan and Millar, Roderick (2004) *Start Up and Run Your Own Business*, Kogan Page.

Reuvid, Jonathan and Golzen Godfrey (2004) *A Guide to Working for Yourself*, Kogan Page.

Schiffman, Stephan (2003) *Cold Calling Techniques That Really Work*, Adams Media.

Southon, Mike and West, Chris (2002) *The Beermat Entrepreneur*, Pearson Education Ltd.

Other brilliant books to stimulate your mind:

Battino, Rubin (2002) *Metaphoria*, Crown Publishing.

Bavister, Steve and Vickers, Amanda (2004) *Teach Yourself NLP*, Hodder Headline Ltd.

Beck, Aaron (1976) *Cognitive Therapy and the Emotional Disorders*, International Universities Press.

Carson, Richard D. (1990) *Taming Your Gremlin – A Guide to Enjoying Yourself*, HarperPerennial.

Chopra, Deepak (1996) *The Seven Spiritual Laws of Success*, Bantam Books.

Covey, Stephen R. (1998) *The Seven Habits of Highly Effective People*, Simon & Schuster.

Covey, Stephen R., Merrill, Roger and Merrill, Rebecca (2001) *First Things First*, Simon & Schuster.

Gawain, Shakti (2002) *Creative Visualization*, New World Library.

Goleman, Daniel (1998) *Vital Lies, Simple Truths*, Bloomsbury.

Holden, Robert (1999) *Happiness Now*, Hodder Mobius.

Jeffers, Susan (1997) *Feel the Fear and Do it Anyway*, Rider.

Kelly, George (1963) *A Theory of Personality –The Psychology of Personal Constructs*.

Kline, Nancy (1998) *Time to Think*, Cassell Illustrated.

Lawley, James and Tompkins, Penny (2002) *Metaphors in Mind*, The Developing Company Press.

Mitchell, Jack (2003) *Hug Your Customers*, Penguin.

Robbins, Anthony (1986) *Unlimited Power*, Simon & Schuster.

Robbins, Anthony (1992) *Awaken the Giant Within*, Simon & Schuster.

Senge, P.M. (1990) *The Fifth Discipline: The Art and Practice of the Learning Organization*, Random House.

Coaching newsletters

A number of coaching companies offer free subscriptions to email-based newsletters. While the prime purpose of issuing them is to promote the company and encourage you to buy their products and services they often contain some really interesting and useful information. We've listed a few to get you started:

Association for Coaching
www.associationforcoaching.com

Coaching Insider
www.coachinginsider.com/

Coach U
www.coachu.com

Corporate Coach
www.brefigroup.co.uk

Coach Daily
www.coachdaily.com

International Coaching Federation
www.coachingfederation.org

Voice of Coaching
www.voiceofcoaching.com

Articles and resources online

There are hundreds of forms free from CoachVille at www.coachingforms.com, and an extensive and awesome set of lists, notes and articles at the CoachVille Knowledge Base at http://topten.org

Some excellent articles on coaching from a cognitive behavioural perspective can be found at: www.centreforcoaching.com/articles

There are over 2000 superb business articles at www.articles911.com; over 675 topics covered at www.mapnp.org/library – a non-profit management library; and tons of business material at www.about.com/business

Arond-Thomas, Manya (2004) 'Resilient Leadership for Challenging Times', *Physician Executive*, July–August.

Hay & Mcber (2000)) 'Leadership That Gets Results By Daniel Goleman', *Harvard Business Review*, March–April.

Noer, David M. (1999) 'When it doesn't work: The Big Three Derailment Factors in a Coaching Relationship'.

Tools of the trade

If you want to win work as an executive coach, get yourself qualified to use a profiling tool. There are many on the market and you need to find the right one to suit your purpose. Becoming licensed to use these tools can be expensive so it's worth choosing one that is flexible and can be used in lots of different situations. Don't just look at the fee for training. You need to calculate the ongoing cost of materials too. We've included just a few for you to consider:

MBTI provides an introductory workshop, a comprehensive guide and a starter pack of materials. There's a compulsory follow-up workshop six to eight weeks later where you get the chance to discuss your experience of using it. Website: www.opp.eu.com/solutions/psychometric/portfolio.asp

Firo-B training covers using the instrument for both individual and team development. You get a manual and a starter pack of materials for around £1000. www.opp.co.uk/solutions/psychometric/firo_b.asp

Extended DISC provide a range of courses which cost from £175 plus VAT. There's a points system for ongoing purchase of profiles. The software package is included. Website: www.extendeddisc.co.uk

Contact us!

Coaching has been an extremely rewarding and satisfying part of both Amanda and Steve's lives. We've seen the tangible difference coaching makes to other people and acknowledge and thank all our teachers and clients for the learning they have so freely given. We know that your competence as a coach will continue to evolve and grow. We would like to thank you for allowing this book to be a small part of that process.

If you have questions about coaching or comment you'd like to make about this book you can contact the authors on either info@speakfirst.co.uk or coaching@infinitepotential.co.uk. We'll do our best to give you a personal reply to any queries you may have.

What you can do

- Choose one book to read from our recommended reading list per month.
- Join a coaching forum and contribute to the future success of the coaching industry.
- Get out and network with other coaches.

Note:

The publisher has used its best endeavours to ensure that the URLs for external websites referred to in this book are correct and active at the time of going to press. However, the publisher has no responsibility for the websites and can give no guarantee that a site will remain live or that the content is or will remain appropriate.

Accountability Where the coach holds the client responsible for things they say they would like to do. The coach usually enquires about progress at the next session.

Active listening Attending to the voice tone, pitch and volume, not just the words people say. Giving someone your full attention.

Authenticity Being true to oneself, behaving in a way that's aligned with core values and beliefs.

Beliefs Generalized ideas that we consider to be true, usually acquired. Guiding principles we use to provide direction in life.

Bottom-lining Encouraging a client to be concise and succinct by personal example and through the use of questions that get to the essence of what the client has to say.

Business coaching Working with business owners on aspects of running a company, including strategy and planning.

Career coaching A specialist who works with people who wants to find fulfilling work that suits their character, previous work experience and that meets their aspirations.

Closed questions Questions that invite a one-word response such as 'Yes' or 'No'. Best avoided in coaching unless confirmation of information given is required.

Coaching A collaboration that assists people in clarifying what they want and achieving their goals through the use of active listening and powerful questioning.

Coaching relationship The partnership between a coach and a client which continues to adapt and develop based on feedback; sometimes known as a 'designed alliance'.

Completion session Final meeting between the coach and client; used to consolidate learning, celebrate success and agree future action.

Conversational coaching Informal coaching carried out in everyday situations using coaching skills.

Counselling Working with people to overcome long-term problems that are rooted in the past.

Curiosity A mindset where the person (or coach) is interested to find out and explore more about a situation or issue.

Deep listening Attending not only to the words someone says but to the way they say them and the emotional quality, energy and emphasis placed on what they say.

Designed alliance A coaching partnership where both parties take responsibility for making the relationship effective.

Directive approach Where a coach acts like a teacher or trainer, advising the client what to do.

Empathy Understanding and imagining what it's like to be in another person's position.

Executive coaching Working with business executives and senior managers to clarify and attain goals.

Experiments Trying a new behaviour or carrying out an action on a trial basis.

Extended DISC Profiling tool used to gain a deeper understanding of individual and/or team behaviour.

Firo-B Tool for measuring how one person behaves with others; assesses interpersonal styles.

Funnel technique Where questions asked initially are broad in scope and then narrowed while still letting the client drive the direction of the discussion.

Goal Something a person is aiming to achieve; the direction in which energy is placed in order to attain something; a stage of the GROW model.

Gremlin Inner voice or 'internal critic' that intends to be supportive but proves counter-productive.

GROW A model created by Sir John Whitmore for use in coaching. Stands for Goal, Reality, Options and What will you do?

Habits Everyday behaviours that are repeated – often outside conscious awareness; structures that give order and shape to our lives.

In-company coaching One-on-one discussions that are carried out by managers and other internal coaches with their clients within organizations.

Intake session The first meeting between a coach and a client in which the coach explains how coaching works and what the client can expect.

Integrity Honesty, and adherence to principles and values that a person holds dear; doing what you say you will do.

Interrupting Where the coach intrudes while the client is speaking with the intention of cutting short a lengthy story.

Intuition Trusting a 'gut' feeling while working with a client, and sharing it with them.

Leading question Enquiring about something in a way that encourages the other person to reply in a particular way.

Life coaching Working with someone to enhance the quality of either an aspect of their life or their life as a whole.

Limiting belief Generalization made about things a person considers to be true that holds them back in some way from achieving what they want.

Mentoring Where a more knowledgeable person passes on what they know and advises someone less experienced.

Metaphor Thinking about or describing a situation in terms of something else such as a symbol or some other representation that implies a comparison.

Myers Briggs Type Inventory (MBTI) A profiling tool that helps people understand the basis of their personality and how this affects their interpersonal relationships.

Neuro-Linguistic Programming (NLP) The study of the structure of subjective experience. 'Neuro', the brain/nervous system; 'Linguistic', language, and 'Programming', the interaction between the brain and language. Founded by Richard Bandler and John Grinder. Their first book was *The Structure of Magic* (1975, Science & Behaviour Books).

Non-directive approach Using listening and questioning to assist another person in understanding themselves better and fulfilling their potential in a way that empowers them to take responsibility for ongoing self-discovery and learning.

Open questions Questions that allow the person responding to choose the direction of conversation and the content of the reply.

Options Choices or possible actions that a client can take to resolve a problem or move them forward towards achieving a goal; a stage of the GROW model.

Perceptual positions Experiencing situations from our own perspective (first position), that of another person (second position) and from a detached position (third position).

Pre-coaching questionnaire Document containing questions that a client completes prior to commencing the coaching relationship, which stimulates their self-awareness.

Reality Client's current situation explored to uncover obstacles and to increase clarity; a stage of the GROW model.

SCORE model Developed by Robert Dilts and Todd Epstein in 1987 and known for it's flexibility. Stands for Symptoms, Causes, Outcomes, Resources and Effects.

Skilled Helper model Developed by Gerard Egan, this has three stages: identifying the problem; understanding the desired outcome; and clarifying action to be taken.

SMART Acronym used in goal-setting. Stands for Specific, Measurable, Achievable or Agreed, Relevant and Time-bound.

Therapy Method of dealing with psychological or social disorders; usually carried out in one-on-one sessions over a period of months.

Training Way of passing on knowledge and skills to others; learning usually takes place with groups and can be delivered to individuals.

Transference Where experiences from childhood are re-enacted with others in present relationships.

Values Something that a person considers to be important; a primary source of motivation behind behaviours.

Visualization Forming images, sounds and feelings in the mind's eye.

Well-formed outcomes Rules for creating the result we want from our actions; stated in the positive with sensory-based evidence of success, within your control to achieve, and ecologically what you want.

What will you do? Sometimes known as the 'way forward' or actions people take to move forwards with a goal; a stage of the GROW model.

Work-life balance Maintaining an even distribution of effort and hours between work and home life.

appendix

This appendix contains a range of useful resources that you can add to your coaching tool-kit.

Intake forms

Sample coaching agreement

Client's name:

Coach's name:

This agreement, between the coach and the above-named client will begin on DDMMYY and will continue for a minimum of three months with each session being of 1½ to 2 hours' duration. It is anticipated that during the contracted coaching period the coaching sessions will take place at approximately fortnightly intervals or as otherwise agreed with the client.

The fees for this coaching will be due for payment on the last day of each calendar month throughout the coaching period.

The services provided by the coach to the client will be carried out face to face or by telephone, as agreed jointly with the client. Coaching, which is not advice (although suggestions may be offered), therapy or counselling, may address specific personal projects, business success, or general conditions in the client's life or profession. Other coaching services include value clarification, brain-dumping, identifying plans of action, asking clarifying questions and making empowering requests.

The final coaching session will be used for completion and review of progress made. At this stage the client may decide to engage the coach for further coaching on a session by session basis.

The coach promises the client that all information provided to the coach will be kept strictly confidential and no details will be discussed with anyone, including the business sponsor.

Throughout the working relationship the coach will engage in direct and personal conversations. The client can count on the coach to be honest and straightforward in asking questions and making requests. The client understands that the power of the coaching relationship can only be granted by the client and the client agrees to make it a powerful relationship. If the client believes the coaching is not working, the client will communicate this and take action to return the power to the coaching relationship.

Our signatures on this agreement indicate full understanding of, and agreement with, the information outlined above.

Client .... Date ....

Coach .... Date ....

Pre-coaching questionnaire – life coaching

Please take time to answer the questions on the following pages. Some of the questions capture information about your current situation. Others will get you thinking about what you want from your coaching sessions. This information will set a good foundation and allow you and your coach to move forward more rapidly.

Please send your coach a completed copy of this form before your first meeting.

General

Name _____

Address _____

Telephone number _____

Email address _____

Birthday _____

Spouse/partner's name _____

Children's names _____

Coaching

What do you want to make sure you get from your coaching sessions. What is your primary focus for being coached? Identify the areas you want to focus your attention on. Be specific about what you want and describe how you will measure your success.

Primary focus

1.

2.

3.

How will you know when you've achieved what you want?

What do you want from your life in the future?

What's important to you in your life?

What activities have most meaning for you?

What do you do when you're really up against it?

Pre-coaching questionnaire – executive coaching

Please take time to answer the questions on the following pages. Some of the questions capture information about your current situation. Others will get you thinking about what you want from your coaching sessions. This information will set a good foundation and allow you and your coach to move forward more rapidly.

Please email a completed copy of this form to your coach before your first meeting.

General

Name _____

Company address _____

_____

_____

Work telephone number _____

Fax number _____

Email address _____

Job title _____

Brief description of your current job _____

_____

_____

_____

Time spent in this role _____

Length of service at this company _____

_____

Coaching

What do you want to make sure you get from your coaching sessions? What is your primary focus for being coached? Identify the areas you want to focus your attention on. Be specific about what you want and describe how you will measure your success.

Primary focus

How will you know when you've achieved what you want?

What do you want from your work/career in the future?

What's important to you in your work?

What work-related activities have most meaning for you?

What do you do when you're really up against it?

Wheel of Life

Each segment of the wheel of life represents an area of your life such as physical environment, personal development, money/finance, family and friends, partner/spouse, fun and leisure, work and career and health and fitness.

1 Use the boxes to label each segment with an area of your own life that's important to you. The centre of the wheel represents little or no satisfaction with that area of your life and the outer rim represents total satisfaction.

2 On a scale of 1 to 10 (where 1 is low satisfaction and 10 is high), rate your level of satisfaction with each aspect of your life.

3 Draw a line across the segment to represent how satisfied you are with that area of your life at the present time, and place the number next to it.

We'll discuss this 'snapshot' of your life experience during the first session. Whatever issue you want to work on, it provides a good starting place for us to better understand how you feel about life as a whole.

See example below:

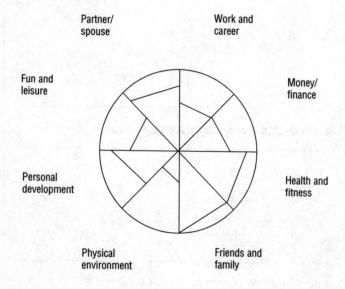

Wheel of Work

Each segment of the wheel of work represents an area of your work such as time management, leadership, delegation, teamwork, planning and budgeting, managing change, communication and problem solving. The topics will vary from person to person.

1 Use the boxes to label each segment with an area of your work that's important to you. The centre of the wheel represents little or no satisfaction with that area of your work and the outer rim represents total satisfaction.

2 On a scale of 1 to 10 (where 1 is low satisfaction and 10 is high), rate your level of satisfaction with each aspect of your work.

3 Draw a line across the segment to represent how satisfied you are with that area of your work at the present time, and place the number next to it.

We'll discuss this 'snapshot' of your work experience during the first session. Whatever issue you want to focus on, it provides a good starting place for us to better understand how you feel about your work as a whole.

See example below:

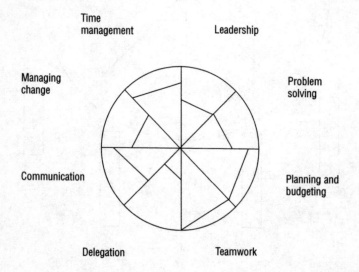

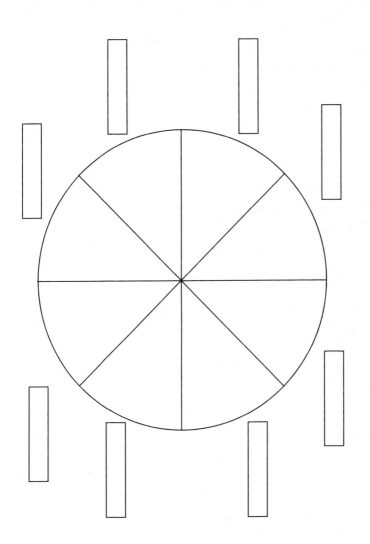

Values elicitation exercise 1

Think for a moment about what's important to you in your life. Jot these initial thoughts down. Then think about the qualities you consider important in others and yourself. Make a note of these too. Finally, ponder over what drives you crazy, and add those things to your list.

Identify your top five values. Then rank them – 1 is most important to you and 5 least important.

1

2

3

4

5

Define your top five values.

To do this, follow the example below.

Example:

'If I was demonstrating this value to my closest friend, this means that I would be ...'

For instance, value = compassion

Definition: 'If I was demonstrating compassion to my friend, this means I would be willing to forgive him or her for making a mistake.'

Value	Definition

Values elicitation exercise 2

Look at the list below and use the 'most' column to tick **five** values that are the most important for you **at work**. Use the 'least' column to tick any values that are really not important to you at all.

Personal values or things that are important to you	most	least
Accountability (reliability, doing what you say you will do)		
Achievement (attaining goals, accomplishment)		
Advancement (progress, promotion)		
Adventure (taking risks, new and challenging experiences)		
Autonomy (working independently, minimal direction from others)		
Caring (compassion, affection)		
Challenge (stimulates full use of your potential)		
Change/variety (varied, frequently changing responsibilities/settings)		
Competitiveness (striving to win, being the best)		
Co-operation (collaboration, teamwork)		
Creativity (being imaginative, inventive, original)		
Economic security (steady, adequate income)		
Freedom (independence, autonomy, liberty)		
Friendship (close relationships with others, rapport)		
Helpfulness (assisting others, improving society)		
Inner harmony (being at peace with yourself and others, tranquillity)		
Integrity (honesty, sincerity, standing up for beliefs)		
Intellectual status (being regarded as an expert in your field)		
Involvement (participating with and including others, belonging)		
Knowledge (understanding gained through study and experience)		
Order (organized, structure, systematic)		
Personal development (learning, strengthening, realizing potential)		
Pleasure (fun, enjoyment, good times)		
Power (influence, importance, authority)		

	most	least
Recognition (respect from others, acknowledgement, status)		
Self-respect (belief in your own abilities, self-esteem)		
Trust (dependability, reliability)		
Wealth (abundance, getting rich)		
Wisdom (discovering knowledge, insight)		

Rank your top five values, where 1 is most important and 5 least important.

1

2

3

4

5

Define your top five values.

To do this, follow the example below.

'If I was demonstrating this value to my team, this means that I would be ...'

For instance, value = control

Definition: 'If I was demonstrating control to my team, this means that I would be monitoring what each manager was doing.'

Value	Definition

Marketing and sales

Mailshot letter sample

Adapted from the Jane Smart letter – see the website www.topten.org/janesmart.htm from Coach University.

Dear .....

I am keen to let you know about my new role as a personal and professional (*Executive/Business/Specialist*) coach.

As you may know, coaching has received quite a bit of media attention recently. In fact, the emerging profession of coaching was mentioned on (*insert details of article, TV or radio programme*). Coaching has received this positive attention because of the success of the clients who use a coach. Here is a brief sample of what the media has said about coaching:

(*Insert two or three quotes here*)

Clients use a coach for any of the following reasons, and often a combination of them:

- To turn a challenging situation around in record time.
- To update or expand people's vision of what it's possible to achieve.
- To make substantial personal changes, including stress reduction and lifestyle simplification.
- To become a much better manager of people.

So, as you can see, coaching is for those individuals and groups who see value in having a confidential partner to challenge them to expand their thinking, resulting in smarter decisions and increased productivity. Coaching has emerged as a consistently effective way of working.

How much do coaches charge? Most charge £?? per hour. My hourly fee is £??. I offer a free introductory session of individual coaching to you or to anyone you know. This gives the person a feel not just for coaching, but to see how well they respond to coaching. Call it a test drive if you will, but I think it's an excellent way to get started and accomplish a goal while you're at it.

I have enclosed a copy of my brochure and business card, and look forward to hearing from you soon.

Warmest regards,

Your name
Coach.

Sales action sheet

How many clients do I have now?	10
How much income do I get from them on average each month?	£1000
How many clients do I really want?	20
How much income do I want to make each month	£2000
What would that increased income do for me?	I would cover my overheads and have some left over to invest in my coaching practice.
What is my goal for this week?	To get another two clients.
What actions will I take?	Send out 20 introductory letters. Attend at least one networking event. Make 30 follow-up calls to my current contacts. Visualize achieving my goal.

NLP
steve bavister & amanda vickers

- Are you new to Neuro-Linguistic Programming?
- Do you want to understand what makes others tick?
- Are you seeking clearer goals, more effective communication and better relationships?

NLP gives you straightforward access to understanding Neuro-Linguistic Programming – one of the most powerful forms of applied psychology available today – and helps you to put the ideas and techniques into practice in both your personal and professional life. If you would like to be more effective, connect with people more easily, and have the opportunity to live your dreams, this book is for you.

Steve Bavister and **Amanda Vickers** are Master Practitioners of NLP and Certified NLP Coaches.

| teach yourself | **running your own business**
kevin duncan |

- Are you planning to work as a freelancer or sole trader?
- Are you struggling with the realities of working on your own?
- Do you need advice and guidance on how to manage your time?

Running your own Business offers you 110 practical ways to ensure independent success. Learn how to motivate yourself, adopt effective habits and – crucially – stay sane, while enjoying your independence and making your business a success. Lots of books tell you how to deal with the practicalities. This one tells you how to deal with yourself.

Kevin Duncan worked in large companies for twenty years and has been working on his own as a marketing consultant for the last five.

flexible working
carol elston and sue orrell

- Are you looking for alternative working practices?
- Are you considering returning to work after a break?
- Do you need some practical advice?

Flexible Working meets today's growing need for a range of flexible work options by focusing on the practical aspects: the technology, tools, mind set and resources required. Whether you work from home, in an office or remotely, you'll feel comfortable negotiating a flexible working package and using the latest technology to support you.

Carol Elston and **Sue Orrell** are Co-Directors of Change Associated Training Solutions Ltd, training people to complete complex business tasks flexibly and effectively using IT, and have co-authored numerous IT and ICT training books.

training
bernice walmsley

- Do you want to improve the performance and motivation of your employees?
- Do you need more confidence in running training sessions?
- Are you planning a training needs analysis?

Training gives you the crucial skills to ensure that your business becomes – and remains – competitive in today's aggressive markets. From analysis and course design to effective presentation and follow-ups, this book offers practical advice to help you plan, build and deliver a training programme to maximize the potential of your business and your staff.

Bernice Walmsley has over twenty years' experience in sales and marketing and psychometric testing. She now works as a freelance writer.